RAILS AROUND BELFAST

An Irish Railway Pictorial

Andrew Crockart and Jack Patience

MIDLAND

An imprint of
Ian Allan Publishing

Rails Around Belfast: An Irish Railway Pictorial
Andrew Crockart and Jack Patience © 2004

ISBN 1 85780 167 9

First published in 2004 by Midland Publishing
4 Watling Drive, Hinckley, Leics, LE10 3EY, England.
Tel: 01455 233 747 Fax: 01455 233 737
E-mail: midlandbooks@compuserve.com
www.midlandcountiessuperstore.com

Design and concept
© 2004 Midland Publishing and
Stephen Thompson Associates

Midland Publishing is an imprint of
Ian Allan Publishing Ltd.

Printed in England by Ian Allan Printing Ltd
Molesey Road, Hersham, Surrey, KT12 4RG.

Front cover: **The historic view was taken on
11th August 1947 at 10.30am as V class
4-4-0 No 83 *Eagle* departs from Great
Victoria Street with the first non-stop
'Enterprise' express for Dublin. The GNR
introduced the new service following
rumours of a plan to set up an air service
between the two cities.**
John Harcourt collection

Rear cover: **W class Mogul No 100 *Queen
Elizabeth* makes a spirited departure from
York Road station in Belfast with a heavy
train bound for Londonderry on 19th April
1955.** H C Casserley

Title page: **Some of the NCC W class 2-6-0s,
displaced from their own lines by the onset
of dieselisation, found employment on the
former GNR system, in the years after the
Ulster Transport Authority took over the
operation of the remaining GNR routes in
Northern Ireland. In this photograph taken
in 1959, No 91 *The Bush*, nears Finaghy
with a Belfast bound local service.**
Jack Patience

CONTENTS

	Introduction	2
1	The Great Northern	6
2	The Belfast Central Railway and the Dock Lines	24
3	The Northern Counties Committee	33
4	Belfast & County Down	47
5	Rails Through the Streets	63

INTRODUCTION

When Ireland's second railway, the Ulster Railway, opened from Belfast to Lisburn in 1839, although the fastest growing community in nineteenth century Ireland, Belfast was still just a town, not achieving city status until 1888. Jonathan Bardon in his book *Belfast an Illustrated History* relates that the town was in festive mood when, on 12th August 1839, 'thousands gathered to watch the opening of the Ulster Railway… the Directors of the Company ignored the warning given by the Presbytery of Belfast that wickedness and vice would result if passengers were carried on Sunday'. Much of the UR's capital was raised locally with the government contributing a paltry loan of £20,000. Passengers and freight were carried, and the enterprise quickly prospered. Dargan also built the Dublin & Kingstown, Ireland's first railway, which, unlike the Ulster Railway, carried passengers only. There was another more fundamental difference between the two. The D&K was built to the British standard gauge of 4ft 8½in, much narrower than that of the Ulster which adopted the 6ft 2in gauge recommended by the government appointed Irish Railway Commissioners. The Commissioners' attempt to spare Ireland the chaos of competing gauges across the Irish Sea came to naught when the Dublin & Drogheda decided in the early 1840s to adopt a gauge of 5ft 2in. The Board of Trade was called in to arbitrate and its inspecting officer, Major General Pasley, struck a compromise at 5ft 3in which was to become the Irish standard gauge.

Work in the north east kept William Dargan, the great Irish railway builder, busy in the 1840s. Railway mania had taken off in Ireland. Dargan's part in building the railways of Ireland could be compared with that of Thomas Brassey in Britain. Dargan, who trained as an engineer under Thomas Telford, was as astute a businessman as he was accomplished an engineer. In Belfast he was busy reconstructing the harbour, laying out the course of the Belfast & Holywood Railway, later part of the Belfast & County Down system, as well as building lines to Ballymena and Carrickfergus for the Belfast & Ballymena Railway.

With the arrival of the railway, old Georgian Belfast had begun the transformation from provincial town to a bustling busy industrial city with large shipyards, a world famous linen industry and heavy engineering factories to rival the great industrial centres in Britain. Indeed, Belfast soon ranked third, after London and Glasgow in industrial development.

The railways soon expanded; the UR reached Armagh in 1848 though through running to Dublin was not possible until the viaduct over the Boyne was completed in 1853. The Belfast & County Down reached Bangor in 1865 and Newtownards shortly afterwards. By 1850 the three terminal stations in Belfast were

in place although it was some years before Queens Quay station, on the far side of the River Lagan, was finally finished.

The B&B, which renamed itself in 1860 the Belfast & Northern Counties Railway, had its engineer, Berkeley Deane Wise, design a splendid terminus at York Road, though unfortunately for the traveller, this imposing building was a mile from the centre of the town. However, transport to both Queens Quay, which was on the far bank of the River Lagan, and York Road was made more convenient when the electric trams ran regular services to both stations, spurs taking them right into the station concourse. Great Victoria Street station, the UR and later Great Northern Railway station, was well placed near the town centre.

There were many plans floated to deal with the one gap in Belfast's railway network, namely a line linking all the stations. Despite little encouragement from the existing railways, the Belfast Central Railway company was formed to build a line from a junction just outside Great Victoria Street station, skirting the edge of the town to reach Oxford Street, where it joined the Belfast Harbour system to connect with the BNCR at York Road. A new bridge over the Lagan allowed through running to the BCDR lines and the interchange of freight between the three systems. In addition, a passenger service between Great Victoria Street, Queens Quay and the Central Railway's terminus at Oxford Street, very close to the present Waterfront Hall, was begun. Unfortunately the sharp curves on the harbour lines prevented through passenger workings to York Road, though, for a short period in the 1920s, the Northern Counties Committee, the successor to the BNCR, ran a service to meet the cross-channel steamers.

The BCR opened for business in 1875 using its fairly basic terminus at Oxford Street and running to Central Junction where it met the Great Northern, with stations at Ormeau Road and Shaftesbury Square. There is no record of passenger trains running to the BCDR at Queens Quay. The developing Belfast horse tram system proved to be the BCR's downfall, attracting potential passengers away with a much more convenient service. The BCR was a commercial failure but it provided a useful link between the three other companies serving Belfast. A central station, which had originally been part of BCR plans, was eventually realised over 100 years later when Northern Ireland Railways revived the Belfast Central line and built Belfast Central station on the banks of the Lagan. In 1885, the BCR was bought by the Great Northern, successors to the Ulster Railway who ran it successfully as a goods link. From time to time, during the summer, Sunday school and other excursions used the line. These popular trips, known to railwaymen as 'the bucket and spade' specials ran to Bangor and other seaside resorts on the County Down system.

The citizens of Belfast, as they hurried around their increasingly busy streets, seemed

This V1 class 0-6-0, No 13 of the NCC, is running on one of Belfast's most useful but least known lines, the Belfast Central. The BCR, which opened its link line between the three main line termini and the docks in 1875, was not a financial success. The Great Northern took it over in 1885 and it became an essential part of the city railway system. Every day hundreds of tons of freight and scores of cattle were carried along its tracks. Irwyn Pryce

blissfully unaware of how fortunate they were to have their railway system connected, unobtrusively, to the docks. There were no level crossings in the town streets. The old Central line carried thousands of tons of goods away from the docks, skirting the busy Belfast streets, with no disruption to its citizens whatsoever. Nowadays, the docks are no longer linked to the railway and heavy goods lorries clog the roads.

The tram service which so effectively choked the fledgling BCR was introduced in the 1870s. There had been horse drawn omnibus services running between the stations and the hotels for some time. These were private ventures funded by the hotels themselves and for the benefit of their patrons. The horse trams, also privately owned, were an attempt to give Belfast a public transport system, despite the opposition of the railway companies, who saw competition to their newly developing suburban train services. When all the agreed routes were established, the tram company owned 94 trams and 800 horses. There was also a steam tram which ran from Whitewell to Cavehill, in the north of the town. This was run by a different company. The horse tram lines were built to 5ft 3in gauge, later converted to 4ft 8½in. Belfast was one of the last cities in the UK to convert its trams to electric traction. This disruptive change took place in 1905, a year after the city authorities had taken over the system. The handsome city power station, built opposite today's Central station, was extended to provide electricity for the new electric trams. Some of the horse trams were converted to electric traction and the Corporation launched an extensive training scheme to retrain the horse car drivers. The training school was in the new tramway headquarters at Sandy Row where large workshops were built on a site alongside the old Central Railway. The poor old BCR still had the ominous shadow of the trams looming over it. Other depots were built in strategic parts of the city, some in the leafy suburbs, others tucked away in the back streets to be discovered with delight by small boys wandering around years later, trying to work out where the trams slept at night.

The system now reached the city boundaries, which considerably worried the railway companies. When there was talk about extending beyond the city limits to Holywood, a route which would have directly paralleled the BCDR line, that company started a much more

intensive rail service to ward off the threat. That line was not built, although the tram route to Balmoral ran very close to Adelaide and Balmoral stations on the Great Northern line to Lisburn.

The Belfast tram system was extensive and covered the city comprehensively. Fares were cheap and from time to time new trams were introduced named after the Corporation's transport manager of the time, who usually had a hand in designing them. There was the Moffett, the Chamberlain and the streamlined McCreary cars. Some of the old open-top horse trams, which had been converted to run on electricity, were further rebuilt to enclose the upper deck. At least one such converted horse tram was still used at peak times in the 1950s; a tribute to its sound construction.

By the 1930s, Belfast Corporation like many other municipalities, was falling out of love with the tram. It decided to replace it with electric trolleybuses. The first trolleybus route opened in 1938 serving the Falls Road. Plans to expand the trolleybus network were disrupted by the gathering war clouds which meant that Belfast's tramways had a stay of execution.

Like so many tram and trolleybus networks on these islands, those in Belfast were ultimately supplanted by the diesel bus which offered a cheaper and more flexible alternative. The last trams ran in 1954, the trolleybuses, once favoured as the replacements for the trams, ran for the last time in 1968 and since then, the city's public transport has been run entirely with diesel buses. Hopes that trams may someday return, perhaps on the abandoned BCDR line to Dundonald, have yet to be fulfilled.

The three railways serving Belfast prospered. By 1914 they were efficiently run, dividends were paid and passengers filled the trains. Goods services ran to every outpost where railway horse and cart services were on hand to deliver right to the customer's front door. The old Central Railway was busy night and day like some giant conveyor belt feeding

the great factories and moving the produce of Ulster's farms. Steam locomotives could be heard clanking around the docks marshalling trains in the small hours. The GNR had built extensive cattle yards at Maysfields, on the site now occupied by Belfast Central station. Most evenings, hundreds of cattle were driven the quarter mile from Maysfields to the cross-channel steamers bound for Glasgow and Liverpool. Laganbank Road echoed to the clatter of hundreds of cattle which arrived from all over Ulster and as far away as Sligo and Mayo.

Lines now served the docks on both sides of the river. Those on the County Down side served the coal quay. Ireland used huge quantities of coal and, and apart from the modest amounts produced by the few indigenous mines, most of this had to be imported from Britain. Steam engines driving the linen mills consumed vast quantities, much of it delivered by rail, and of course the products of these factories were brought back to the docks for export. The lines on the County Down side of the river also connected with Harland & Wolff's extensive railway system, which served the various works and fitting-out basins. In the early days, Harland's usually hauled their loads around the yards with a steam crane which could also load and unload as required. However, in the 1930s, when ship orders were sparse, H&W began to build some of the first diesel shunters. The NCC and BCDR made use of some of these.

There were few sidings in the Belfast area serving local industry; customers of the railway seemed content to collect and deliver their consignments direct to the railway premises or have it done by the railways' cartage service. However, just after the end of the Second World War, as part of the government's drive to attract new industry, Courtaulds built a large textile plant at Carrickfergus and installed a private railway complete with two Peckett shunters to move the large quantities of coal which such an operation needed. This line lasted into the 1970s and was only removed when Courtaulds closed down. Nearby, Carrickfergus harbour was also rail connected. Although close to Belfast this small harbour seemed to thrive until the 1950s; perhaps their rates were more reasonable than those of 'big brother' nearby. As well has handling general merchandise, Munster Simms, the oil distributor, had a depot there which delivered fuel all over the province, much of it by rail. Rivals Esso had a Belfast depot which was connected to the Harbour lines.

While the Great Northern works in Dundalk looked after the heavy engineering needs of that railway, the company's locomotive shed at Adelaide, a mile from Great Victoria Street station, was the largest in Ireland. It had space for 55 locomotives under cover and had extensive servicing facilities. A large contingent of drivers, firemen, cleaners and over 50 fitters were employed. There was also a workshop for wagon and carriage repairs. The BCDR had its works at Queens Quay. However the most extensive workshop facilities in Belfast were at York Road where the day to day business of maintaining, servicing and building rolling stock was carried out alongside work on the design of locomotives. For many years the BNCR's locomotive engineer was Bowman Malcolm. Appointed to this prestigious position at the age of 22, he completed over 50 years service before retiring in the early 1920s. York Road works are still in use today, as the major engineering centre for Northern Ireland Railways. The old BNCR also designed and built many handsome and unusual station buildings. Some, happily, are still with us today. They developed major tourist attractions which sometimes involved considerable engineering works such as the cliff path at Whitehead. New residents in these growing outer suburban areas like Whitehead were attracted by low season ticket rates and other clever inducements.

Despite this, the development of suburban traffic into Belfast was mainly confined to the Great Northern and the County Down. There were fewer suburban station on the lines out of York Road; for many years the first station out from the terminus was at Greenisland, six miles away. The 1850s saw both the Great Northern and the County Down expand their short-haul services and open new intermediate stations to serve the ever-expanding town. In 1851 Belfast had 97,784 residents; by 1901 this had risen to 349,180 and to 386,947 in 1910. Early services used conventional locomotive-hauled trains, but cost-conscious management's saw ways of saving money by trying out railcars and railmotors. The BCDR successfully ran local services to Holywood, on the Bangor branch and Dundonald on the main line, using Kitson-built steam railmotors. These quaint machines lasted until after the 1914 war and were popular with travellers. Fares were collected by conductors and the service was frequent. The Bangor branch being level to Holywood was suitable for these low-powered units. The Great Northern bought steam railmotors for the Lisburn service but they were

never considered very successful, being replaced by auto trains and push-pull workings. This method of operation meant that the locomotive did not to have to run round its carriages at the terminus. The County Down also started operating auto trains, when the lack of servicing and high mileages accumulated during the First World War left the Kitsons railmotors worn out. The NCC, successors to the BNCR, tried Sentinel steam railcars in the 1920s, a type which had proved reasonably successful on other railways. These had been taken out of service by 1930 to be superseded by diesel railcars. Perhaps the heavy gradients to Antrim and Ballyclare which defeated the earlier experiments had proved too much for the Sentinels as well.

Ireland led these islands in the development of diesel rail traction. In the 1930s, the BCDR acquired two diesel locomotives from Harland & Wolff. These machines mostly ran on the Ballynahinch branch. The Great Northern at Dundalk built two railcars in 1932. The NCC's first railcar, a petrol driven machine built in 1933, was followed in 1934 by the first of several diesel railcars. These experimental early cars ran successfully for many years. Ultimately their success led to the construction of express buffet car trains for the Great Northern, delivered in 1950. It was quite a few years before British Railways followed their example. York Road works, by then in the hands of the Ulster Transport Authority, produced diesel trains for the Bangor line and the former NCC lines in the 1950s.

The period covered by this book begins roughly in 1930 when all three railways running into Belfast were fending off competing private bus services and the ever-increasing use of the private car. To deal with this threat, the railways bought out the bus companies and ran the services themselves co-ordinating road and rail time tables. They also speeded up services with new and more powerful locomotives hauling modern coaches built to the latest designs. Great Victoria Street station saw the first of the new Great Northern compound locomotives arrive at the head of a speeded-up Dublin to Belfast express service. The NCC acquired the first of its W class 2-6-0 locomotives from Derby and introduced new coaches of modern design. Both railways invested heavily in civil engineering works to allow faster running. The Great Northern rebuilt the Boyne viaduct and the NCC, with help from the Northern Ireland government, was able to build the impressive viaducts at Bleach Green which avoided the necessity of main line trains having to reverse at Greenisland. This was something that company had wanted to do for many years. The NCC and the Great Northern now ran the fastest services in Ireland. The County Down carried on running its line in much the same way it had done for many years, not troubled by the modernising flurry of its neighbours.

In the early 1930s the two larger railways suffered from bitter and long drawn out strikes

which crippled services and soured working relations. Meanwhile, the Northern Ireland government was increasingly worried about the whole transport situation, particularly the potential danger of ill-maintained private buses racing, unregulated, around the roads, creaming off money from the harassed railways. While many of the competing bus services were being bought by the railways, the carrying of goods remained unregulated. After much consultation, the government formed the Northern Ireland Road Transport Board which was charged with running all buses and road freight services in the province. Under the legislation setting up the new Northern Ireland Road Transport Board, the railway companies were no longer allowed to run buses and lorries. Those they possessed had to be handed over to the NIRTB. The hapless railway companies were given shares in the new board, but no money. A pooling system was designed to balance road and rail finances. Bus and rail services were to be co-ordinated. Unfortunately the NIRTB failed to live up to the hopes of its creators, losses were high and co-operation between road and rail did not happen.

The railways' fortunes were transformed by the huge demands placed upon them by the Second World War. Heavy troop trains ran, freight train tonnage increased to cope with war production and petrol rationing virtually wiped out private motoring. The Great Northern carried thousands of people to the Republic where food rationing was not in force and many luxury goods were available. Smuggling, a part of life since the division of the island in the 1920s, flourished even more due to wartime shortages. The NCC although not an international line like the Great Northern, reached the border at Derry, and with its joint interest in the narrow gauge County Donegal Railway gained much traffic from those seeking relief from wartime economies. The air raids on Belfast forced many people to move outside the city each evening, and return for work the next morning. The railways coped with this increase in traffic despite the constant threat of enemy bomber attacks. In the hope of avoiding unnecessary damage by enemy action, the NCC moved its coaches from the yards in Belfast to country sidings each night. This happened every night except, inexplicably, on the evening when German bombers struck York Road station wiping out the inward goods shed and most of the station façade, wrecking the overall roof and destroying over 20 coaches and 200 wagons.

The war suspended further discussion about the state of the transport system. However, new legislation was in place by 1948 and the Ulster Transport Authority was formed to preside over road and rail transport in the province. The Great Northern was excluded as its lines crossed the border. The BCDR, now a gentle and old-fashioned railway, which could not afford the pre-war modernisation schemes of the other two companies serving Belfast, was in a rundown state. The new Ulster Transport Authority acted decisively and closed the entire BCDR main line despite the fact that the section from Queens Quay to Comber carried a lot of commuter traffic. This hasty decision was encouraged by an increasingly anti-rail government.

The Great Northern was in financial difficulties by the early 1950s. To keep services running, the governments north and south of the border bought the company in 1951 and in 1953 set up the Great Northern Railway Board to run it on their behalf. The GNRB lasted until 1958 when its assets were equally divided between the UTA and CIE, the Republic's nationalised transport undertaking. Unlike the passing of the old railway companies, no one seemed unduly upset at the demise of the Ulster Transport Authority in the late 1960s. Buses, railways and freight were split into three separate independent companies under a Transport Holding Group.

Close observers of government antipathy where railways are concerned, detected a gleam of hope in the 1970s when the fledgling Northern Ireland Railways bought a new 'Enterprise' train together with some diesel multiple units for suburban services, relaid the old Central line, built Belfast Central station and rebuilt the bridge over the Lagan. The old

When the Belfast Corporation tram system was electrified in 1905, this large workshop was built along with a depot at Sandy Row to cope with the new trams. The electric tram drivers school was in the same building. The works remained in use with little alteration until the last tram ran in 1954.

BCR ambition of a central station for Belfast had become reality. It was now possible to join the Bangor line with the main line to Dublin. Derry trains were diverted through Antrim and Lisburn to reach the new station, though this added 20 minutes to the running time. It was a few years before the second cross-harbour bridge allowed the Larne line access to Belfast Central and the Derry trains to use the former NCC main line to reach Belfast Central. The price paid for all this rationalisation was high; Belfast lost all three of its original terminals.

In the late 1990s, the main line to Dublin was relaid with EU assistance and new trains bought. NIR was merged into a new holding company, Translink, which also operated Ulster's bus services. Some positive developments have occurred under the new regime such as the restoration of Carrickfergus station. As in the old days, the stationmaster, now area manager, is in charge of road and rail in the area. Bangor has a new station, and Coleraine a rebuilt one, and that at Lisburn has won an award.

Perhaps growing patronage of the railways (Dublin line traffic has increased by 50% in the last few years) will encourage those in charge to maintain the system properly and avoid the uneven investment policy which, in the past, has been the cause of so much difficulty in running the system properly. At present services are run with railcars over 25 years old though new rolling stock is on the way and at last, the Bangor line has been relaid. However, as railways expand across Europe, the shadow of closure hangs over the Derry line and the Larne branch beyond Whitehead. Sensible people feel that we have lost too much of our railway system already and are convinced

that lines under threat should be given a chance to show how they can perform when investment puts them in a position where they can meet the challenge. The expanding greater Belfast area needs its railways more than ever as we enter the new century.

Acknowledgements and Thanks
Many persons have been cajoled into helping with this book. Particular thanks are due to Charles Friel, who has given freely of his time and put at our disposal his unique archive covering Irish railways from the very beginning. Desmond Coakham and Derek Young were close to the project and their extensive memories, wisdom and considerable personal collections helped to keep us on the rails so to speak. Richard Whitford, John Laird, Norman Foster, Richard Casserley, Des Fitzgerald, James Friel, Ian Sinclair, Tony Ragg and John Harcourt allowed us to dig deeply into their collections for new treasures as did John Kennedy, Mark Kennedy, Norman Johnston, Clifton Flewitt, Colm Flanagan, Len Ball and Bill Scott. Pearse McKeown, a former GNR man, has the sort of memory normally connected to a computer and was invaluable in checking details. Friends in both the Irish Railway Record Society and the Railway Preservation Society of Ireland were also generous with their help. Mike Maybin, an authority on Belfast's trams and trolleybuses provided much help with that part of the book and Craig Robb, equally at home with ships and trains, provided insight into the Harland & Wolff shipyard's rail system. Without the generous and expert help of so many, our task would have been almost impossible. Our apologies if anyone has been inadvertently omitted from the foregoing. All photos not acknowledged are from the authors' collection.

THE GREAT NORTHERN

GREAT VICTORIA STREET

Above: **A view of Great Victoria Street station, the terminus of the Great Northern Railway, in 1900. This was always Belfast's best located station, a few minutes' walk from the City Hall. Trains arrived and departed from here from the 1840s until the station was closed in the 1970s with the opening of Belfast Central station. Common sense later prevailed and a new station was opened here in the 1990s for suburban services at least, if not the Dublin expresses.**

Left: **A view of part of the concourse at Great Victoria Street station. With the partition of the island in the 1920s, this became an international station which added a touch of the slightly exotic to the place, which the other Belfast termini lacked.**

Top: **The Traffic Manager's offices for the whole Great Northern system were in the old Royal Irish Constabulary building at the corner of Glengall Street and Great Victoria Street. This view was taken from a rear window of that building and provides an unusual perspective on the station and its overall roof. In the distance the large sheds of Grosvenor Road goods depot can be seen.** Charles Friel collection

Centre: **This historic view was taken on 11th August 1947 at 10.30am as V class 4-4-0 No 83 *Eagle* departs from Great Victoria Street with the first non-stop 'Enterprise' express for Dublin. The GNR introduced the new service following rumours of a plan to set up an air service between the two cities. Customs examinations, which normally took place at the border, were carried out at each end of the journey.** John Harcourt collection

Below: **The 5.30pm weekdays Belfast to Dublin 'Enterprise Express' leaves No 5 platform for its 2¼ hour sprint to Dublin. This Dublin based unit was the first inter-city diesel express in these islands. The Belfast based service remained steam hauled for some time. With a refreshment bar taking up considerable space in the centre coach, additional seats were needed. Whilst work went on to convert another trailer, to cope with the overflow in the interim, the authors remember a freshly painted mahogany grained clerestory coach being attached to the rear of the unit. First class passengers had a panoramic view through the driving cab and relaxed in Pullman-style seats with meals being served to them.** David Odabashian

Top: **Platform 1 at Great Victoria Street,** outside the protection of the station's overall roof, was known as the motor platform from the time when the steam railmotors, introduced to improve suburban services in the face of tramway competition, used it. On the right are the catering department's stores. and behind the buffer stop is the control office for the northern section of the railway. S class 4-4-0 No 171 *Slieve Gullion*, prepares to depart with the afternoon train to Warrenpoint on 3rd January 1953.
E M Patterson

Centre: **V class 4-4-0 No 85** *Merlin* in the original lined black livery applied to these engines when they were first introduced, is about to depart with the 8.15pm up Dublin mail, on 1st June 1932. As built, these locomotives had round-topped fireboxes. The box on the footplate was part of a modification to their lubrication system needed to cope with problems created by their higher than normal boiler pressure of 250psi. Behind the train is the original 'Boyne' bridge, carrying Durham Street over the tracks, which was extensively rebuilt later in this decade. William Robb

Bottom: **On 13th May 1950, standing quietly in the sunlight at Great Victoria Street is one of the GNR T2 tanks, while PP class No 44 waits underneath the rebuilt 'Boyne' bridge with the 5.35pm to Warrenpoint.**
H C Casserley, courtesy Charles Friel collection

Top: **No 28 was built for the BCDR in 1937
by Harland & Wolff. She outlasted the poor
old BCDR by several decades. This diesel
locomotive worked on both the NCC
system and here at Great Victoria Street on
the former GNR. The breakers finally
caught up with her in 1974, just a year after
she retired.** Charles Friel collection

Centre: **This strange looking eight wheeled
diesel hydraulic locomotive was supplied
by the German firm of MAK to the GNRB in
1954. Numbered 800, she trundled round
most of the system in the careful hands of a
German fitter and the great Paddy Mallon
from Dundalk works. While not an
unqualified success and lacking brake
power, she managed to prove herself
competent. One apparently obvious critical
observation made at the time of her first
appearance was the locomotive's long
coupled wheelbase. She was fitted with a
patent system which allowed her to
negotiate quite tight curves. When the
GNRB was dissolved, she passed to CIE who
did find the long wheelbase a problem at
some locations. At the time of writing, it is
believed that bits of her survive as a power
unit in a County Galway scrap depot. In
this view No 800 is shunting at Great
Victoria Street.** David Odabashian

Bottom: **Near the end of steam working on
the former GNR system, we see S class
No 174 *Carrantuohill* at Great Victoria
Street, with her fireman looking reflective
as he waits for the signal which will allow
her to trundle gently down the third road
and home to Adelaide engine shed after a
strenuous trip from Dublin with the
2.45pm semi-fast on a frosty February
evening in 1964. She was to be cut up the
following year. Behind No 174 and standing
on the site of the carriage sidings and
platform 5, are the Ulster Transport bus
offices.** Paul Riley

Above: **On 21st July 1959, VS class 4-4-0 No 209, *Foyle*,** is seen leaving Great Victoria Street with the 3.00pm to Dublin. Behind the locomotive is a full Brake to cope with the Great Northern's extensive sundries business. Murray's tobacco factory, on the right, provided one of the defining smells of this station. The other distinctive odour was Dunville's distillery about half a mile further on near the railmotor shed. The distillery was long gone but the tobacco factory was still there with its exotic smell of imported leaf. E M Patterson

Below: **Adjacent to the passenger station was the GNR's Grosvenor Road goods** depot. Apart from cattle, all Great Northern goods trains, including a large amount of Guinness traffic, were dealt with here. On the right of the picture, Harland & Wolff-built diesel locomotive No 28 shunts the yard. Many of the large sheds remain and are now part of Grosvenor Road Business Park.

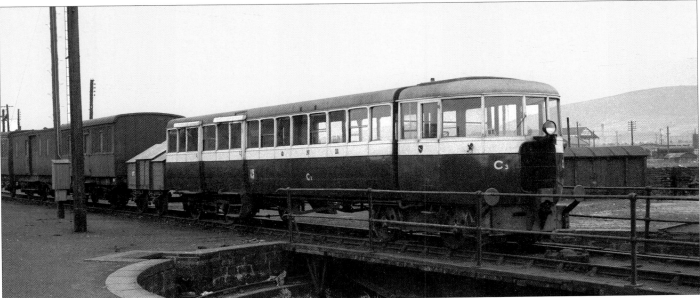

Top: **UG class 0-6-0 No 49 (GNR locos which came to the UTA were renumbered, this is the former GNR No 149), is seen on 28th July 1958 at the newly installed turntable at Great Victoria Street on the site of the the original Ulster Railway locomotive shed. This was the start of a scheme to attempt to create a small locomotive facility here which may have allowed the UTA to close Adelaide shed.** E M Patterson

Centre: **When the GNR's Derry line closed, various pieces of rolling stock not generally seen in Belfast arrived for storage. Here railcar C₃ is at Great Victoria Street complete with her lightweight luggage trailer. On the Derry Road she provided local services.** Jack Patience

Bottom: **This strange angular machine worked for years in Grosvenor Road goods yard. Built by Rapier, it loaded and unloaded containers. In this official GNR photo, it is swinging a bread container from road to rail. The GNR pioneered the movement of bread from the main Belfast bakeries across the province. The local breadman loaded his van directly from the container. These containers were built at Dundalk and painted in the colours of the various bakeries.** GNR(I)

Above: **This view shows the outer limits of Great Victoria Street yard near Central Junction. U class 4-4-0 No 66 *Meath* is shunting bread containers. Passing by on a local service are railcars Nos 6 and 7, the UTA's very first railcars, acquired in 1951. Converted from pre-war Third class coaches, they proved successful and led to the building of the various classes of railcar for which the UTA became well known. Mechanically they were similar to the AEC units of the Great Northern. The shed on the left in the background was built many years before for the maintenance of the steam railmotors. From the 1950s it was used to service the AEC railcars but was always known as the 'railmotor shed'.**

Left: Belfast Central Junction with the 1.30pm goods from Portadown, hauled by an unidentified ex-NCC W class 2-6-0, negotiating the crossover to the third line before entering Grosvenor Road goods yard. The signal cabin to the right has gone but the junction remains. The Belfast Central line ran off to the right behind the cabin.

ADELAIDE SHED

Top: **An impressive line-up of locomotives is seen outside Adelaide, the GNR's largest locomotive shed, in 1933. A V class compound is under the sheer legs, on the left of the picture, with a sister locomotive on the track next to these. Other locomotives which can be identified include a couple of T2 4-4-2 tank engines. The elevated building on the far right is the coaling stage. Further to the right (out of sight) was a wagon repair facility.**
Ian Allan Library

Centre: **A line-up of Great Northern locomotives at Adelaide, in a view dating from the 1958/1960 period, before NCC locomotives became regular inhabitants of the shed. The engine nearest the photographer, one of the first batch of the U class 4-4-0s dating from the period of the First World War, carries a 'UT' stencil on its buffer beam. To the right of the U class are a T2 4-4-2 tank, an SG3 class 0-6-0 and another U class.**

Bottom: **A former NCC WT class 2-6-4 tank, commonly known to railwaymen and enthusiasts alike as 'Jeeps', an indication of their ruggedness and versatility, simmers quietly outside the the doors of Adelaide shed. At its peak, there were over 50 fitters employed here. Latterly, it must have been a draughty place to work in, particularly when the doors rotted and were removed.**
Derek Young

Top: **SG3 class 0-6-0 No 33 hangs disabled under the sheer legs at Adelaide. These attractive and long lasting locomotives, among the most powerful 0-6-0s ever to run in Ireland, had driving wheels of 5ft 1in diameter which gave them a good turn of speed when they were employed on passenger duties. The GNR V class Compounds were frequently seen dangling from these sheer legs having attention to their valves due to lubrication problems which could cause a build-up of carbon.** Desmond Coakham

Centre: **No 151 of the seven strong PG class was originally painted green and called** *Strabane.* **Built in 1899, she lasted until 1961, not a bad innings. Her tender is certainly not the one she started life with in Dundalk where she was built all those years before.** Jack Patience

Bottom: **As the suburbs of Belfast expanded, the GNR opened more stations to cater for these communities. To work such suburban services economically, many railway companies in the early twentieth century tried various types of steam railmotors. These incorporated a small steam locomotive into a passenger coach. This GNR railmotor, No 2 built in 1905 by R & T Pickering, was powered by a steam engine made by the North British Locomotive Company in Glasgow. The railmotor could be driven from either end and was able to haul a trailer. These units lasted until 1913 but were not considered a great success. However, with the steam units removed, they were converted to run as conventional carriages and in this form they lasted until the end of the steam era.** Charles Friel collection

Opposite page:

Top: **PG class No 10 takes coal at Adelaide. The coal wagons were pushed up an incline and small trucks called boxes were used to feed the locomotives. No 10 spent a lot of her time shunting the docks.**

Bottom: **1936 built Railcar E is parked at the not often photographed south end of Adelaide shed. Railcars D and E were powered by a six coupled unit in the centre of the vehicle. Having the power unit there, articulated from the two coaches, virtually eliminated vibrations and smells from the diesel engine penetrating the passenger saloons. Along with units F and G, this was the final development of the GNR's pioneering articulated railcar designs. E was broken up in 1961.** Both, Jack Patience

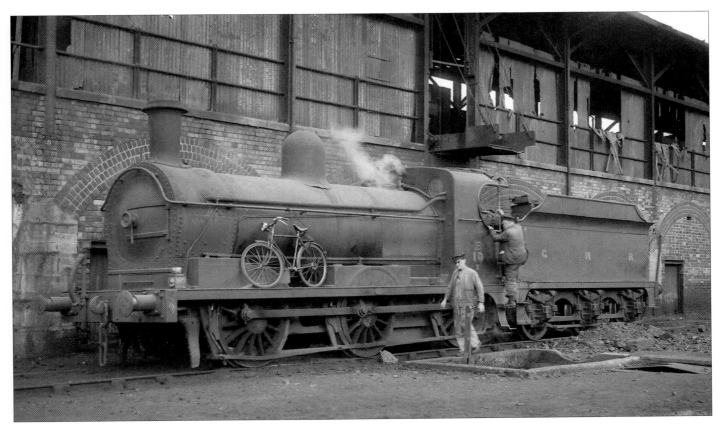

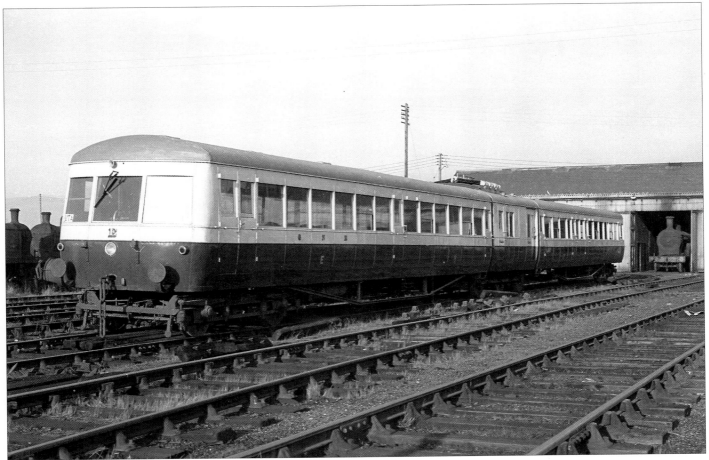

ADELAIDE STATION

Above: **An unidentified T2 class 4-4-2T is seen approaching Adelaide with a mixed set of vehicles of both GN and NCC origin, probably forming the 5.43pm service to Antrim. The houses on the right front onto the appropriately named Great Northern Street, home of many railwaymen.**

Left: **Another class T2 tank, No 139, is seen at Adelaide station on a local service to Lisburn. There were two types of these versatile and nippy tank engines, the T1 and T2 classes. These tank engine versions of the U class 4-4-0s were built between 1913 and 1925 by Beyer Peacock and Nasmyth Wilson. The festoon of telephone lines overhead served the Great Northern's wartime Wagon Control Office on the left-hand platform.** Charles Friel

Above: **When the Great Northern Railway Board was abolished in 1958, and the remains of the system were split between the UTA and CIE, the diesel locomotives which were rapidly taking over from steam south of the border began to appear on the GNR main line. Here a green liveried MetroVick diesel A11 hauls the Dublin bound 'Enterprise' past Adelaide. The stock is a set of Bulleid designed CIE Park Royal coaches whose doors were inset to keep within the loading gauge.** Jack Patience

Right: **The MetroVick diesels proved very unreliable in service so CIE turned to the American firm of General Motors for its next batch of locomotives. On 4th August 1961, a Dublin bound express passes Adelaide hauled by a brand new GM diesel, B131, in the grey and yellow livery which they carried at first. These single cab 950hp GM units were rather underpowered and often worked in multiple. Today the 201 class GM diesels hauling these trains have 3,500hp at their disposal!** E M Patterson

Top: **In June 1959, V class 4-4-0 No 85 *Merlin*, coupled to a VS tender, is passing Adelaide with the returning Thursday shoppers' excursion to Dublin. Frequently three or four trains were needed to cope with this traffic. Adelaide's two footbridges can be seen in this view. The far one served Adelaide engine shed. Although it was little used by the staff, generations of railway photographers found it an ideal vantage point.** Jack Patience

Centre: **The footbridge mentioned above was used to good effect to record this view of the 3.00pm semi-fast to Dublin with WT class 2-6-4 No 57 hauling a set of CIE coaches. The Dublin service is passing a down goods train, including empty bread containers, which is heading for Grosvenor Road goods depot. Adelaide engine shed's water tower dominates the background.** Charles Friel collection

BALMORAL

Bottom: **Balmoral was an attractive small suburban station with a loyal middle class clientele. However, every spring, Ulster's largest agricultural show at the nearby showgrounds thrust extra business upon it. This is a special returning to Enniskillen on 25th May 1956, full of farmers and their wives, at the start of the long run back to Fermanagh. Ps class 4-4-0 No 72 is in charge. Hidden behind the train, there was a fan of sidings to accommodate the livestock traffic at show time.** Drew Dondalson, courtesy Charles Friel

FINAGHY

Right: **S class No 192** *Slievenamon* brings a Belfast bound mid-morning goods from Portadown past Finaghy signal box. To cope with the huge increase in traffic during the Second World War, two sidings were installed here at that time.

Below: **VS class No 59 (GNR No 210)** *Erne*, passes though Finaghy at the head of a heavy rugby excursion bound for Dublin. It is a great shame that none of these engines, the last 4-4-0s built anywhere in the world, were preserved. Her train consists of ex-Great Northern coaches. The first vehicle is a Tri-composite built for the Dublin to Derry service, the second one is an all First from the original 'Enterprise Express' stock while the third vehicle is a Buffet car finished in the railcar blue and cream livery. The rest of the set consists of Dundalk-built flush panelled stock.
Both, Jack Patience

DUNMURRY

Left: **S class No 63 (GNR No 192)** *Slievenamon*, is passing Dunmurry level crossing with the 8.00am Portadown to Belfast commuter train on 3rd July 1961. Just behind the train is Meeting House crossing which saw so many unpleasant accidents before being turned into a pedestrian only facility. J D Fitzgerald

Below: **U class No 66** *Meath*, a member of the 1948 batch, is seen leaving Dunmurry on the 5.35pm to Antrim. The 'W' sign reminding drivers to sound their warning devise, was to protect the notorious Meeting House crossing mentioned above.
Jack Patience

DERRIAGHY & LAMBEG

Above: **No 68,** *Down,* recorded here near Lambeg, was another one of the post-war U class with the larger and square windowed cab which gave better protection to the crew but did nothing to improve the engines' aesthetic appearance. These later locomotives had a higher pitched boiler to allow the cylinder and valve block casting to be strengthened but they were not as handsome as the first batch.

Below: S class No 173 *Galtee More* passing the accommodation crossing between Lambeg and Derriaghy. For many years, Sam McGreedy's Rose Garden was a familiar, fragrant and colourful spectacle beside the main line at this location.
Both, Jack Patience

LISBURN

Top: **On 6th May 1959, T2 tank No 30 slips over the crossover and into Lisburn station with a local from Belfast. This was one of the last of these engines to remain in service.** Ian Allan Library

Centre: **An unusual interior view of Lisburn signal cabin. It is a distinctive building with wings built on either side to assist sighting. Alec Davidson is the man pulling the levers.** Victor Corrie

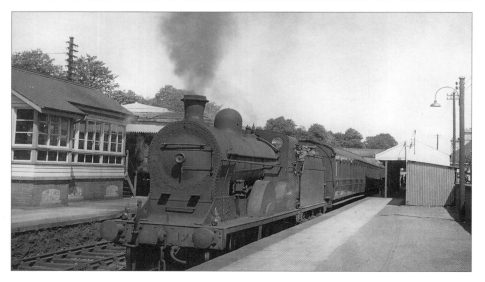

Bottom: **The wings on the signal cabin mentioned above can be seen in this view of Lisburn station. Unusually, at Lisburn the cabin was situated on the island platform. The signalman has a good view of S class No 171 *Slieve Gullion* and her Portadown bound train which stand opposite the signal cabin awaiting the Guard's whistle. This interesting building is still in place though it is now used by permanent way staff. The corrugated iron building on the platform is one of the Great Northern's bicycle sheds.** Ian Allan Library

KNOCKMORE JUNCTION

Top: Knockmore signal cabin was built in 1887 to the design of W H Mills, chief engineer of the GNR at the time. It controlled the important junction outside Lisburn where the lines to Banbridge and Antrim diverged from the Belfast to Dublin main line. Well-known author E M Patterson took this shot from the footplate of WT class No 56 on the 1.10pm from Great Victoria Street to Antrim on Saturday 20th August 1960. Alfie Black was the signalman that day and is preparing to offer the staff for the single track section ahead to the driver of the 'Jeep'.

Centre: **In May 1946, V class 4-4-0 No 84 *Falcon*, passes Knockmore Junction. The locomotive is in the blue livery but still carries its original type of boiler with a round-topped firebox. After the Second World War, all five locomotives were rebuilt with boilers which had square Belpaire fireboxes, similar to those on the later VS class locomotives. The roof of the signal cabin is on the right and two railway houses are behind the smokebox.**
Both, E M Patterson, courtesy Charles Friel

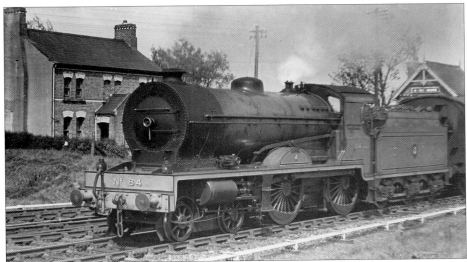

Bottom: **Knockmore Junction from an unusual angle with the cabin hidden behind the train. The Antrim branch is on the left, the truncated Banbridge line on the right. Trailing off it is the long disused siding which had crossed the road and led to a US army base. WT class No 51 hurries by on a Dublin semi-fast.** Jack Patience

THE BELFAST CENTRAL RAILWAY
AND THE DOCK LINES

CENTRAL JUNCTION

Above: **A UG is heading a special down the erstwhile Belfast Central line at Central Junction. The lines in the foreground lead to Great Victoria Street station. Passenger and oil trains were worked over the Belfast Central line on the absolute block system. Goods trains could run under permissive block regulations to speed up the traffic. In the line's heyday, at busy times, as many as six or seven goods trains could be waiting to reach the docks. The leading coach in this formation is a Tri-composite, one of two built for the Derry to Dublin service which would have been detached from a main line train at Portadown to be added to a Derry working.**

Centre: **UG class No 49 is approaching Central Junction with a goods train from Maysfields. Behind the footbridge, on the left, a 1990s-built chord completed a triangle linking Great Victoria Street and Central station with the main line.** Ian Allan Library

Bottom: **No 32, the first UTA multi-engined diesel (MED), is working a football special from Bangor to Adelaide along the Belfast Central line. The unit is passing in front of Belfast City Hospital with the wall of the Belfast Corporation tram workshops and headquarters on the right.** Richard Whitford

MAYSFIELDS

Top: **UTA No 26** *Lough Melvin*, **bought by the Authority in 1959, following the closure of the Sligo, Leitrim & Northern Counties line in 1957, is shunting on the site of today's Belfast Central station.** *Lough Melvin* **and her sister** *Lough Erne* **were built by Beyer Peacock in 1948 for the SLNCR where, in common with the line's other locomotives, they were never given numbers being known by name only. Sister locomotive** *Lough Erne* **was numbered 27 by the UTA.** H C Casserley

Centre: **PG class 0-6-0 No 10 is simmering at Maysfields with a train for the quays. This old workhorse lasted until 1964. All members of the PG class survived into UTA ownership. A gas-holder at Ormeau Gasworks, a feature of the skyline of this part of Belfast for many years, is seen behind the locomotive.** John Laird

Bottom: **One of the Sligo engines, hauling a coal train, is passing Maysfields cattle yards on the right. By this time, the live cattle trade had ended and the cattle platforms are being used to store redundant ex-NIRTB/UTA Leyland Octopus lorries. Beyond is Belfast Corporation's generating station which was built in 1898 and extended in 1905 to cope with the tramway electrification. The fledgling BBC used its chimneys to support their first aerial in 1923.** Derek Young

EAST BRIDGE STREET JUNCTION

Above: **No 44, one of the splendid PP class 4-4-0s of the GNR, was an unusual sight at East Bridge Street Junction working a return special from Bangor to Lurgan. Seen on 31st May 1958, this was only the second recorded occasion since the Second World War when a PP worked to Bangor. The train has just left the 'shaky' bridge over the Lagan, and is passing the vandalised, but still working, East Bridge Street cabin before reaching the site of today's Central station. Officially these locomotives were not allowed over the bridge. The tracks above the first coach lead to the docks and the NCC.** Drew Donaldson

Left: **In this pre-war shot, taken on 28th July 1938, No 197, one of the original members of the U class built in 1915, is hauling a return special from Bangor to Dublin. She is paired with a much larger than usual tender, perhaps borrowed from one of the S class locos, being rebuilt at Dundalk works at the time. The greater water capacity of the bigger tender will be useful for the long run ahead. The S class emerged from the works resplendent in blue livery. No 197 had to wait until after the Second World War for this to happen to her.** William Robb, courtesy Charles Friel

THE 'SHAKY' BRIDGE

Top: **The view from the cab of a UG locomotive as it crosses the 'shaky' bridge from the Queens Quay side of the river towards Maysfields. Officially known as the Lagan viaduct, the condition of this bridge can be imagined from it colloquial name. Only engines with light axle loadings, such as the GNR U and UG classes were permitted to cross it, and dock lines. The gas holder at the Ormeau Gasworks of Belfast Corporation is again apparent.**
E M Patterson, courtesy Charles Friel

Centre: **The 'shaky' bridge, as it was known by generations of railwaymen and enthusiasts alike, had been originally built by the Belfast Central. Its closure in 1965 isolated the Bangor line from the rest of the system. All maintenance work on the MEDs which ran on the Bangor line was carried out at the old BCDR works at Queens Quay. When the new Central station was constructed, a replacement bridge was built which was strong and modern but without the character of the original. When work started on the new bridge, which opened in 1976, the piers of the old bridge were found to go down only 15 or 20 feet and it is related that they were not too difficult to remove. However, in searching for solid foundations for the new bridge, was one area, the contractors had to dig down for some 90 feet before finding solid rock.** John Laird

Bottom: **Former GNR RT class 0-6-4T, No 23, works a train of empty oil tank wagons bound for the Esso depot at Airport Road on the County Down side of the river. This train would have been working under the absolute block system on the Belfast Central line and is trundling down the incline from the 'shaky' bridge towards the junction with the BCDR. The tall building behind is the County Down's locomotive shop and the smaller one was for wagon repairs.** H C Casserley

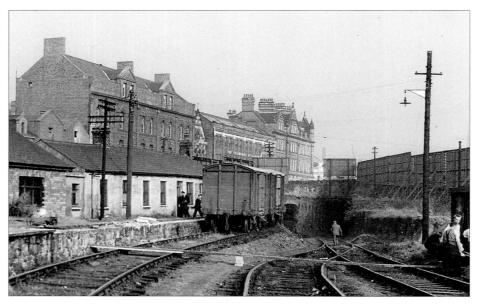

QUEENS BRIDGE

Above: **UTA No 24 (GNR No 166) was one of the four RT class 0-6-4T locomotives specially built by Beyer Peacock for use on the Belfast dock lines. They were designed with squat chimneys and low cabs to allow them access to all parts of the docks and particularly the tunnel under the Queens Bridge. These features gave them a powerful appearance although they were really quite small locomotives. The buildings behind, although railway-like in appearance, were those of the City Morgue. There is evidence of building works on the left Oxford Street bus station was being built at the time.** Drew Donaldson

Centre: **NCC V1 class 0-6-0 No 13 was built in 1923. On 30th May 1963 she is hauling a goods train from East Bridge Street Junction past Oxford Street bus station and will shortly disappear into the tunnel under the Queens Bridge on her way to York Road station, via Donegall Quay. Oxford Street bus station was built on the site of the Belfast Central Railway's Queens Bridge station.** Irwyn Pryce

Left: **Looking in the opposite direction to the picture above, in an earlier view before the bus station was built, we see Queens Bridge station, headquarters of the old Belfast Central Railway. The line on the right leads under the Queens Bridge to Donegall Quay. Clearances under the bridge were tight.** E M Patterson, courtesy Charles Friel

DONEGALL QUAY

Top: **An RT emerges from the Queens Bridge tunnel and is about to pass the site of the old BCR's Queens Bridge station. The Waterfront Hall, Belfast's flagship entertainment venue, is now located here.**
John Laird

Centre: **PG class 0-6-0 No 10 climbs out from the tunnel under the Queens Bridge to emerge on Donegall Quay. There were no fences and people could wander at will. The main destinations for the overnight passenger and freight services which used Donegall Quay were Heysham, Liverpool and Glasgow. By the time passengers arrived to embark, the holds would have been filled and the cattle loaded on board.**
Norman Foster

Bottom: **A typical scene on Donegall Quay with one of the Sligo engines shunting; the large building on the right is the administration offices of the former LMS shipping division. In the evening, after the shunting had finished, intending passengers had to pick their way over the square setts and the embedded track to get to the dismal shed that so long served as the terminal for the cross-channel services.**
Derek Young

DOCK LINES

Top: **The crew bicycle on the footplate was a familiar sight on locomotives working the docks. Similar to many Victorian dock lines, the railway here although close, did not run along the edge of the quay so extra handling was needed to get goods from ship to rail. Here at Donegall Quay a mobile crane helps to solve this problem. In earlier days when there was a lot of small sundries traffic, little electric flat trucks on hard rubber wheels scuttled about the area, bouncing uncomfortably over the square setts and the inset track.** Norman Foster

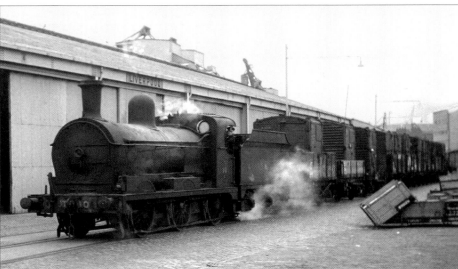

Left: **Great Northern PG No 10 trundles past the cross-channel Donegall Quay sheds with a train of British Railways containers. Much of the goods conveyed to and from the docks in these latter years were in such containers which helped to cut down handling costs.** John Laird

Below: **An NCC V1 class 0-6-0 heads along Donegall Quay past the cross-channel steamer sheds, on its way to the Great Northern's transfer yard at Maysfields. Shortly the train will go through the tunnel under the Queens Bridge. The building behind, on the left, is the headquarters of the former LMS shipping services to Fleetwood and Heysham.** Irwyn Pryce

Above: **RT class No 24 (GNR No 66) is clanking along Donegall Quay with an enthusiasts' train. Everyone is enjoying panoramic views from station seats put in open wagons. It is perhaps difficult to imagine such a casual yet safe way of travel being permitted in today's health and safety conscious society!** Norman Foster

Centre: **This U class 4-4-0 has negotiated the 'shaky' bridge and finds herself on the dock lines on the County Down side of the river. The flagman accompanying the engine is checking to confirm that Queens Road, which she is about to cross, is clear of all traffic. Up to the abandonment of Belfast's tramways in 1954, this 5ft 3in harbour line was crossed by the 4ft 8½in tracks of the Corporation Tramways. In the distance is the spire of St Patrick's church now unfortunately closed.** Craig Robb

Right: **No 29 was an 0-6-4 tank built by Beyer Peacock in 1923 to work the dock lines for the BCDR. She is heading for the coal quay with a load of empties in March 1946. The roads and rails around the quays were owned by the Belfast Harbour Commissioners. No 29 is proceeding with caution down New Channel Road to the junction with Queens Road where the Belfast Corporation trams cross this line on their way to the shipyard. There should be a man with a red flag leading the train but perhaps he is out of the picture on the left.** Desmond Coakham

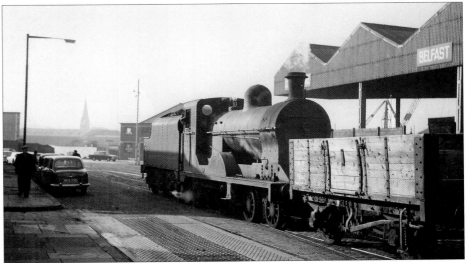

Above: **In 1950 an order for 20 AEC railcars for the GNR began to arrive in both Belfast and Dublin. Looking most attractive in blue and cream livery, here one of the first of these railcars is gently swung ashore at Belfast docks.** John Harcourt collection

Left: **Harland & Wolff had an extensive network of 5ft 3in track which connected to the Harbour railway, and linked their various factories to the slipways and fitting out basins. This picture taken in early 1958 shows the Harland-built diesel shunter supplied in 1933 to the BCDR to work the Ballynahinch line, and later returned. With the centre wheels removed to allow easier passage round the sharp curves in the yard, it is acting as works shunter. Previously heavy loads were moved by a self-propelled steam crane; there is no evidence of a steam locomotive being used. Here the shunter is passing along Queens Road. Behind the 270bhp locomotive is the boiler for the Union Castle Lines ship, *Pendennis Castle,* which plied between Southampton and Cape Town.** Craig Robb

THE NORTHERN COUNTIES COMMITTEE

YORK ROAD STATION

Above: **This, the most imposing of the three Belfast termini, began as a fairly basic structure in 1848 and was improved in 1873-5. Finally in the 1890s, under the guidance of Berkeley Deane Wise, the BNCR engineer, there emerged this classic building with a tram canopy and hotel behind. Inside there were various little chalet-type buildings which served as the ticket office, coffee stall, tobacconist and newsagent.**

Right: **Derby-built W class 2-6-0 No 92, *The Bann*, at York Road at the head of an express in the mid-1930s.** Charles Friel collection

Top: **York Road-built No 95 (later to be named *The Braid*) differed from most of her sisters by having an LMS-type hooter instead of the more usual whistle. She has the earlier small Midland style tender; later Moguls had an LMS tender with increased coal and water capacity.** Ian Allan Library

Below: **Belfast York Road, as very few remember it, showing the original canopies and overall roof. This view was taken in June 1939 just a couple of years before the station would be devastated in the Easter air raids of 1941. A1 class 4-4-0 No 58 was built in York Road in 1907 and rebuilt there in 1934. This locomotive was withdrawn in 1954.** Charles Friel collection

Left: **Approaching York Road on a train from Larne in the early 1930s, No 68 started life in 1908 as an A class before rebuilding in York Road turned her into an A1 4-4-0. On the right is the long-gone carriage shed, another casualty of the 1941 Belfast blitz. The diamond sign on the smokebox door denotes a train from a branch line.**
Charles Friel collection

WAR DAMAGE

Top and centre: **York Road shortly after the disastrous bombing of 5th and 6th May 1941 which severely damaged the station and the railway offices. The goods depot was wrecked and 20 coaches and 250 goods wagons were destroyed. Unusually, the coaches had not been removed that night to a country siding to save them in case of just such an attack, as was normally the case. Many irreplaceable records and drawings were also lost in the raid. After the second raid, the station was unusable and a bus service was organised to Whitehouse and Jordanstown which became temporary termini. After the first bombing, some departments had already moved away from York Road. With help from other railways' works and the Royal Engineers, a wagon reconstruction programme was started. Clearing up and temporary repairs went ahead and the LMS sent over some old coaches which were regauged and put into service.**

Below: **Sometime after the bombings, the offices have been patched up but the great columns have gone for ever. Although the overall roof is being repaired, the station never returned to its former spacious elegance.** All photographs on this page, John Harcourt collection

NCC LOCOMOTIVES

Top: **No 13 was one of the three V class 0-6-0s built in 1923. When they first arrived, the NCC could not decide what numbers to allocate to these machines so they were given the temporary identifications of X, Y and Z! They survived into UTA days when all three were rebuilt. They appeared occasionally on passenger trains and in later days worked regularly in the the docks. Behind No 13, and appearing to have a very large chimney growing from its roof, is York Road power signal box. The whole station was controlled from here. The colour light signals were installed in 1926 and were the first of their kind in Ireland.**
Derek Young

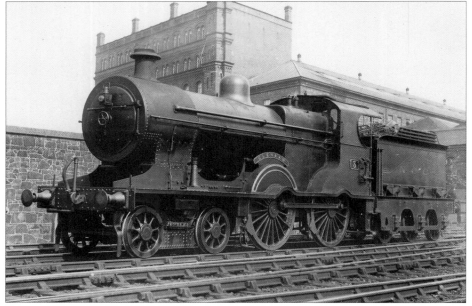

Centre: **U1 class 4-4-0 No 3** *Glenaan* **was built in 1890 to the design of the great BNCR engineer, Bowman Malcolm, as a 2-4-0 compound. It was originally named** *Galgorm Castle*. **The engine was rebuilt in 1931 in the form seen here and remained in service until 1946.**

Bottom left: **Built in 1890 by Beyer Peacock as a compound and rebuilt as class C1 in 1928, this is No 52, seen on 5th August 1930 before her final rebuild to a U1 4-4-0 in 1931 when she was renumbered 4. The NCC locomotive department revelled in these substantial rebuilds and complex renumbering procedures.**

Bottom right: **No 16 was built at York Road works in 1914 and lasted until 1951. A considerable amount of her work was on the Harbour lines where her short wheelbase came in useful. She had a very cramped cab. The bracket on the saddle tank was apparently to assist with holding the hose whilst water was being taken.**
All three photographs, Charles Friel collection

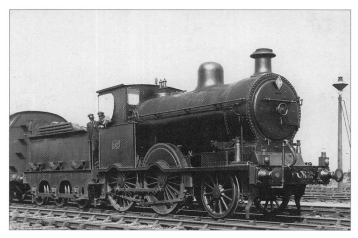

Top: **O S Nock, the famous railway author and train recorder, took this photo of No 81 *Carrickfergus Castle* in 1936. No 81 was built as a U2 at York Road in 1925. From his early visits, Nock recognised the high standard of running and timekeeping which the NCC achieved on a main line that was mostly single track.** O S Nock, Charles Friel collection

Centre: **A pleasant portrait of WT class 2-6-4T No 2 looking reasonably clean and still quite new. As built there was an awkward sharp corner in the side tank plate work where the top of the side tanks met the vertical cab. An ideal situation for the development of metal fatigue, the problem was tackled by introducing a small radius at this point. No 2 has not yet been modified.** Ian Allan Library

Bottom: **Two LMS Jintys, numbered on the NCC 18 and 19, were regauged and transferred from England in 1944 to help ease the shortage of motive power at the time. First rostered on local passenger services, this must not have been a success as their vacuum gear was later removed. They were usually found shunting round the docks and at York Road. No 19 is seen in front of the large Jennymount linen mill. The building with the curved windows, immediately behind the coach, is the engine house which provided power for the looms and all the other machinery. Above is a large water storage tank cleverly blended into the design of the building. The mill was designed by Sir Charles Lanyon, the great local architect who created so much of the Belfast cityscape in the Victorian era.** Ian Allan Library

DIESEL PIONEERS

Top: **Railcar No 1 was designed and built at York Road in the 1930s. Originally equipped with petrol engines, these were later replaced with diesel power units. Mechanical controls were used to link the two driving consoles at either end of the railcar. No 1 is a most significant vehicle, the first railcar with underfloor engines driving through an early torque converter. This historic vehicle survives in store at the Whitehead depot of the Railway Preservation Society of Ireland, where it awaits restoration.** Charles Friel collection

Centre: **'Management interference' is one reason why this ugly vehicle came to be built. Major Spier, the NCC's innovative general manager thought that railcar No 1 (built the year before in 1933,) was rather too heavy so he bypassed the engineering hierarchy and gave the design of this car, No 2, to a young engineer. This is the result. Lighter yes, but it travelled the NCC all its days with a sag which became apparent during construction. Despite this disability, she rattled on to be scrapped in 1954 – the first of these early cars to go. The elevated driving position allowed a trailer to be propelled while still giving the driver a reasonable view of the signals. All these railcars had a lower than normal roof profile to allow for the driving turrets.**

Bottom: **Diesel railcar No 3 owes more of her design characteristics to car No 1 than to her immediate predecessor No 2. She has an elevated driving cab allowing trailers to be propelled. Although this practice ceased after an altercation with a cow on the Portrush branch, No 3 looks very smart here – brand new and sporting a very attractive maroon and cream livery.** Charles Friel collection

Top: **Railcar No 4 was very similar to No 3. All these early railcars had both First and Second class accommodation. No 4 is at the buffer stops at York Road station under the rather utilitarian canopy constructed to give some protection to passengers following the removal of the overall roof which, as was recorded earlier (see page 35), was destroyed during the Second World War. She is standing at the little-used Platform No 4.** Richard Whitford

Centre: **This is one of the diesel locomotives built by Harland & Wolff in an attempt to diversify their output during the economic depression of the 1930s. No 17 was a 330bhp diesel hydraulic locomotive built in 1937. She was the second such machine to be constructed by that great shipyard. At first the locomotive was hired to the NCC who later purchased her. No 17 last worked in 1966 and was scrapped in 1970.**

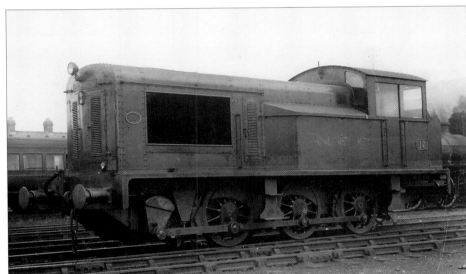

Bottom: **No 16, another Harland & Wolff diesel locomotive, was built by them as a works shunter before passing to the NCC. This locomotive had mechanical transmission. Behind is the NCC's weighing shed.** Charles Friel collection

YORK ROAD
WORKS AND SHED

Top: **On 18th May 1968, 0-6-4T No 27 *Lough Erne* waits as the former GNR weedkilling train has its tanks filled with potent liquids. This train consisted of an ever changing array of ancient converted tenders or old tank wagons. The sprayer wagon was built on the remains of a GNR six-wheeled coach.** Craig Robb

Centre: **WT No 6, seen outside York Road shed, carries the logo of its third owner, Northern Ireland Railways.** Jack Patience

Bottom: **No 27 *Lough Erne*, shunts a goods train in York Road yard. Apart from the main lines in the foreground, this site is now buried under the M2 motorway.** Jack Patience

Photographs on the opposite page:

Top: **Inside York Road works on 11th June 1950, No 93 *The Foyle* and No 99 *King George VI* are sharing the cramped space with a 'Jeep'. These works, now modernised, are still the main NIR workshops.** E M Patterson

Centre left: **York Road shops around 1930; the frames lying on the floor look intended for a 4-4-0 and tender.** Richard Whitford collection

Centre right: **Mogul No 104 receiving attention at York Road works.**

Bottom: **In the spring of 1968 one of the Sligo tanks is standing beside the RPSI's preserved Great Southern & Western J15 class 0-6-0 No 186. Behind is the coaling plant installed in the 1930s when the station and yard were modernised. This was known to staff as 'the Cenotaph'.**

LEAVING YORK ROAD

Above: **A spirited departure from York Road by the now preserved 'Jeep' No 4 hauling a heavy Larne boat train on Christmas Eve 1966. The first vehicle in the train is a 'brown' van. These vacuum braked vans were seen on many passenger workings on the former NCC system. The carriages making up the train include some of the handsome bogie coaches built in the 1930s for the NCC's crack service, the 'North Atlantic Express'. Fortunately, like No 4, one of these carriages has been preserved by the RPSI.**

Left: **'Jeep' No 4 is again the locomotive here, gingerly picking her way over the crossovers at York Road on 31st May 1970. This working was to convey bridge girders for storage at Ballyclare Junction. These would eventually be used to build a bridge to carry the railway over the new M2 motorway. The significance of this occasion is that this is believed to be the last time that an Irish railway operator used a steam locomotive on official duties, as opposed to enthusiast specials. This working was fairly exacting with No 4 leading and No 53 banking. A very steady 20mph had to be maintained up the 1 in 75 climb out of Belfast, without snatching or stalling, to make sure the load was secure. These were the last serviceable steam locomotives on NIR's books.** Both, Craig Robb

Top: **In the winter of 1965 Derek Young captured this evocative shot of WTs Nos 4 and 10 crossing Whitehouse viaduct with an express for Londonderry. The WTs were an interesting mix of LMS engineering. Built after the Second World War, they were essentially a tank engine version of the W class 2-6-0s of the 1930s. They combined Fowler designed boilers, valve gear and cylinders with modern features such as a rocking grate and a self-cleaning smokebox. Their 6ft driving wheels gave them a very good turn of speed.**

Below: **No 10 on a heavy boat train from Larne Harbour speeds past Trooperslane, one of the wooden stations designed for the BNCR by Berkeley Deane Wise. This one has been demolished, but those at Antrim, Carrickfergus and Portrush remain, as attractive today as they must have been when first built.** Richard Whitford

Right: **No 93 *The Foyle*, about to cross Bleach Green viaduct and tackle the stiff gradients on the way to Antrim, was photographed from the footplate of a Belfast bound Mogul as it nears the end of its lengthy run from Londonderry just over 90 miles away. A perusal of the Working Timetable has yielded the interesting information that these two trains are indeed scheduled to pass here. The fact that they do is down to fine running and good timekeeping and reminds us that the NCC was offering some of the fastest times ever seen behind steam traction in Ireland following the introduction of the Moguls in the 1930s.** E M Patterson, courtesy Charles Friel collection

BLEACH GREEN VIADUCTS

Top: **In the early 1930s work began on a new viaduct and flying junction at Bleach Green, near Whiteabbey, about 4¾ miles out from York Road. Trains for Derry no longer had to reverse at Greenisland and could run straight through to Antrim and beyond. The work was heavily subsidised by the Northern Ireland government as a relief scheme to ease the chronic unemployment of the time. Much of the labour force was unskilled and the use of reinforced concrete on such a scale was unfamiliar to railway engineers, so its successful completion was a credit to all involved. Here, the main viaduct, which will carry trains to the north west, is seen under construction.** A H Glendinning collection

Centre: **The works at Bleach Green are seen soon after completion. The main viaduct and its burrowing junctions for the Larne branch brought to an end the time-wasting reversal at Greenisland for all trains heading up the Derry line. It also enabled the NCC to close several level crossings in the vicinity. Here the main line viaduct is on the right while the bridge to the left carries the Larne branch.** Ian Allan Library

Below: **In 1934, No 81 *Carrickfergus Castle* descends towards Belfast with a main line freight. The works cost £250,000 but speeded up main line services by 20-25 minutes. The down Larne line is in the foreground; the siding off this served Henderson's linen works.** Tony Ragg collection

Top: **The Great Northern and the NCC met in two other places apart from the docks in Belfast. In Cookstown they had adjacent stations and here, at Antrim, they shared the same station. The Great Northern branch from Knockmore Junction terminated in the bay to the left of the picture. This line terminated at an engine shed and turntable. The NCC main line to Londonderry is on the right, occupied by a goods train. Both companies ran separate passenger services to Belfast, but the NCC's was by far the shortest and quickest route to the city. On the up side there were sidings used by the Army who had a large local depot and off to the left was an extensive goods yard. The station, built in 1902, was another attractive example of Berkeley Deane Wise's unique style. The building is still in use today.**
Ian Allan Library

Centre: **This place was called Carrickfergus Junction until 1933 when the new viaduct at Bleach Green made reversal here unnecessary. Since then it has been known as plain Greenisland. Before the new bridge was built, all trains for the main line were hauled the six and a half miles from Belfast by smaller engines which were replaced by the express engine which then hauled the train up the steeply graded line (on the right of the picture) to Antrim and beyond. This route, the back line, as it was known, remained in use for many years, mostly for freight but on summer Saturdays a direct Derry to Larne boat train ran. To cope with the new layout, the signal cabin was rebuilt with colour light signalling, electric point motors and track circuiting. This was one of the first instances in the United Kingdom where a signalman was enabled to control movements of trains he couldn't see. The 'Jeep' in this view, taken on 30th December 1963, is No 10.** E M Patterson, courtesy Charles Friel

Right: **A returning empty spoil train passes Greenisland. These were known as the muck or spoil trains and with a 'Jeep' at each end, they shuttled backwards and forwards carrying hardcore between the cement works at Magheramorne on the Larne line and the construction site of the new M2 motorway, which ran parallel with the railway on the approaches to York Road. They were the last steam hauled freight trains in these islands.** S C Nash

CARRICKFERGUS

Above: **This is the well-known preserved Great Northern locomotive No 171 *Slieve Gullion* on her first railtour in the care of the Railway Preservation Society of Ireland. Seen on Saturday 8th October 1966, standing at the up platform at Carrickfergus No 171 gets an admiring look from a young spectator.**

Centre: **On 31st August 1967, WT No 10 waits to depart from the island platform at Carrickfergus with a steam crane to assist in the rerailing of hopper wagons forming one of the spoil trains from Magheramorne to Belfast. With these short-wheelbase four wheel hopper wagons, derailments were not an unknown occurence. The wagons had stiff springs to cope with the heavy loads they carried, which made them rather prone to this sort of accident, particularly when they were running empty.** Both, Derek Young

Left: **The Courtaulds Textile Company's Carrickfergus factory had two Peckett-built tank locomotives. One of the pair is seen shunting wagons near the wagon tippler which is just behind the brick building on the right. The railway closed with the factory in 1968 after just 20 years in existence. Though the two locomotives *Wilfred* and *Patricia* were advertised for sale in the local press, no one came to save them and they were eventually cut up for scrap.** Desmond Coakham

BELFAST & COUNTY DOWN

QUEENS QUAY STATION

Above: **The front of Queens Quay terminus in 1962 after the UTA had removed its attractive and useful canopy. In tram days, a spur swung off to the right and then ran inside the station building, a boon in our frequently inclement climate! Queens Quay was finally closed in 1976 when Belfast Central station was opened.** Charles Friel collection

Right: **The splendid concourse at Queens Quay was the most spacious of all the Belfast termini. It looked at its best when this photograph was taken in the early twentieth century. In its later years the station had five platforms, none too many for the BCDR's busy commuter timetable.**

BCDR LOCOMOTIVES

Top: Almost the whole of the County Down fleet of locomotives was built by Beyer Peacock in Manchester. However, No 28 alias No 9, was built by Sharp, Stewart in 1887. She ran with a tender before being rebuilt as a tank engine and lasted into Ulster Transport Authority days but was never steamed by them. The shed in the background, the railmotor shed, was later used to store some of the exhibits which were to be displayed at the Belfast Transport Museum and, upon its closure, at the Ulster Folk & Transport Museum at Cultra. H C Casserley

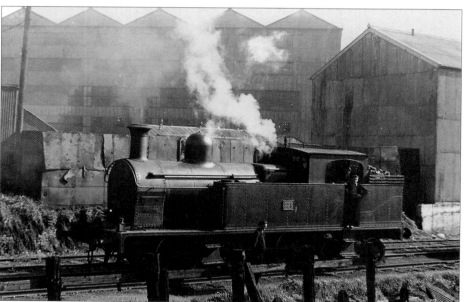

Centre: **This good-looking locomotive is No 29, the only one in her class and designed to shunt the dock lines. She had 5in of play in the middle drivers. No 29 is basking in the sunshine on the link line between the County Down and the docks, which (strange as it may seem) belonged to the Great Northern. Towering behind her are the Engine works of Harland & Wolff where propulsion machinery was built for the world's ships, as well as some pioneer diesel locomotives. Despite her obvious usefulness and a shortage of suitable motive power at the time to operate on the dock lines, this locomotive was nevertheless withdrawn in 1956.**
Charles Friel collection

Bottom: **Waiting at platform 5 at Queens Quay station is 2-4-2T No 7 coupled to a Great Northern panelled coach, slightly different from her normal load of Victorian six-wheelers. With her round-topped firebox and circular spectacle windows she is not quite typical County Down as we came to know it. The BCDR locomotives were nearly all fitted with Belpaire fireboxes and in consequence had an attractive set of oblong spectacle windows which gave them a distinctive appearance.**
Ian Allan Library

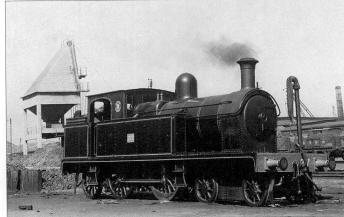

Top left: **Baltic or 4-6-4 tank No 222 in UTA days with her smokebox open and the ash being shovelled out. It seems that these beautiful white elephants were ordered on a director's whim at a time when the company was between Chief Engineers. Despite their lack of performance and heavy coal consumption, the Baltics lasted to the end of steam on the County Down.**

Top right: **Standing in front of the modern coaling plant at Queens Quay is very clean 4-4-2T No 217, awaiting her next turn of duty. She is one of the smaller 4-4-2 tanks which were probably the most handsome locomotives on the railway.** Both, Charles Friel collection

Above right: **No 6 had a long life and was for many years the BCDR's only true express passenger engine. As such she worked the 'Golfers Express' on a Saturday and in true County Down style, just about every other sort of train on the railway through the rest of the week, although she was seldom seen on the Bangor branch. Built in 1894 by Beyer Peacock, No 6 was overhauled and given a Belpaire firebox in 1943. Renumbered 206 by the UTA, after the 1950 closures she saw little service and was sold for scrap in 1956.** Charles Friel collection

Bottom: **In early Ulster Transport days, Baltic No 223, looking every inch a powerful machine, sits on the road leading past the locomotive offices and into the workshops. Sadly, these engines were not up to the job at all. The UTA transferred No 223 to the NCC. She did not perform any better there; even her downhill running was disappointing.** Ian Allan Library

QUEENS QUAY WORKS

Top: **A portrait of the staff at Queens Quay works taken on 14th April 1933. This was shortly after the end of the crippling railway strike which affected the NCC and the GNR badly. On the BCDR, the men took the pay cuts proposed by the management and carried on working.**

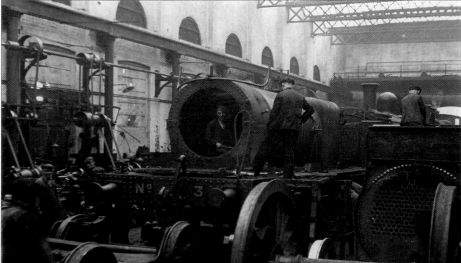

Centre: **Standard tank No 3 undergoing heavy repair in the BCDR's Queens Quay works in May 1946. In 1965, when the Bangor Line was truncated by the Ulster Transport Authority, these works maintained the diesel fleet until the new Central station opened in 1976. After this the works remained as a maintenance depot for NIR's permanent way vehicles until plans for a new Lagan bridge and approach road forced its demolition. When the works finally closed, the overhead crane of 1878 vintage was saved and proved a useful addition to the new workshop at the RPSI depot at Whitehead.** E M Patterson

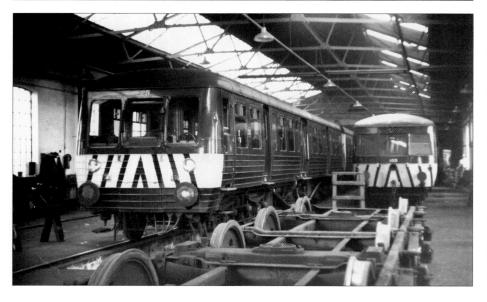

Bottom: **The old and new side by side in Queens Quay diesel maintenance depot. On the left is MED (multi-engined diesel) No 25, built by the UTA at Duncrue Street works in 1952. These railcars had automatic sliding doors operated by the guard. They were also fitted for multiple operation, something the AEC cars on the Great Northern lacked. This is the accepted reason for the UTA developing a separate railcar design. However, as first built their performance was dismal and new gearboxes were fitted in 1968. These were built by Walter Wilson of Self Changing Gears who also built the boxes for the GNR's first railcars as well as the AEC units and many similar British Railways vehicles. Wilson was born in Dublin and among his other pioneering work he invented his pre-selector gearbox in 1901. Its first significant use was in the British tanks which so shook the German Army when they first appeared. In fact, the War Department credited Wilson as the principal inventor of the tank. Subsequently they were installed by Armstrong Siddeley and Daimler in their cars and buses. For many years the Belfast Corporation bus fleet was dominated by Daimler-built vehicles. Wilson's invention was the precursor of the fully automatic gearbox we use today. Sitting beside No 25 is the early GNR articulated railcar F, renumbered 105 by the UTA. She too has a Wilson gearbox.** Richard Whitford

LEAVING QUEENS QUAY

Top: **This is No 13, one of the smaller 4-4-2 tanks, leaving platform 5 which was known as the Holywood railmotor platform. The signal gantry with the neat smoke deflectors is only a taster for the fine gantry which stood astride the main lines further along the station throat.** Ian Allan Library

Centre: **In County Down times, Baltic No 22 towers over a BCDR standard six-wheeler, as she enjoys attention from her driver. Neither drivers nor firemen were fond of these hulks. They ate coal, so the crew called them 'miner's friends'. Alas, having scoffed the coal, they failed to deliver the power.** Ian Allan Library

Bottom: **This wonderful view is of one of the large tanks, No 8, in BCDR days, leaving Belfast. It shows what a beautiful proscenium arch the signal gantry makes. This gantry was the most impressive at any of the three Belfast termini.** H C Casserley

THE MAIN LINE

Top: **This shows the interior of Ballymacarrett Junction signal box after the severing of the line to Comber and Newcastle. The panel above on the left related to the County Down's automatic banner signalling system on the Bangor line. An illustration of one of these distinctive signals is on page 57. Installation of this started in the 1920s and finished some ten years later. This system lasted until 1976.** Charles Friel collection

Centre: **Seen in the sunshine at the long-closed but then very well kept Dundonald station, is BCDR 0-6-0 No 26 at the head of a long excursion train. This locomotive spent much of her time on the Donaghadee branch working both passenger and goods trains. The track bed from Dundonald back to Belfast is intact as far as the Holywood arches, the name of the bridge carrying the railway over the Holywood and Newtownards Roads, about a mile from the city centre.** William Robb

Bottom: **On 2nd January 1950, standard 4-4-2 tank No 13, on the 10.30am from Donaghadee, meets 2-4-0 No 6, hauling the 10.45am to Newcastle at Comber station. Comber, like Holywood, Queens Quay, Newcastle and Bangor, had middle roads which allowed locomotives to run round their trains. This facility made these stations much easier to work at busy times.** E M Patterson

NEWTOWNARDS

Top: **Newtownards station, the second one on the site, was generally thought to be very awkward to shunt. The layout had been entrusted to a young engineer who made a series of mistakes which, unfortunately, future generations of railwaymen had to cope with. The connection to the yard was from a turnout situated in the middle of the down platform face. Nevertheless it was a very busy and prosperous station serving a number of substantial linen mills and a bustling market town.** Desmond Coakham

Centre: **A Donaghadee to Belfast train arrives at Newtownards station on 2nd April 1950. Once this service is on its way to Belfast, the goods at the other platform will be able to shunt the yard. BCDR vans were usually of the convertible type, like the first wagon on the goods. This meant that they could be used for either general goods or livestock. In the Irish climate sealing a leaky roof tarpaulin or cleaning out a wagon after it had been used by animals must have been a daunting job.**

Below: **Newtownards station with a goods train about to shunt before taking the remainder of its train on to Donaghadee. A typical handsome 'pill box'-style BCDR signal cabin gives a comprehensive view of the station. Beside it is a subway linking the platforms and in the foreground is the awkwardly sited point leading to the goods yard.** Both, E M Patterson

THE BANGOR BRANCH

Top: **In the early 1950s shortly after the Ulster Transport Authority took over the County Down, some of the versatile 'Jeeps' were sent from York Road, along with some modern coaching stock, to help the ailing BCDR fleet. They were popular with the crews and well suited to the work. No 10 makes a grand exit from Queens Quay under that distinctive signal gantry.** Charles Friel collection

Centre: **The Irish Cup Final was being held at The Oval, home of Glentoran FC, and a special, headed by one of the light ex-GNR UG class 0-6-0s, one of the few types which were permitted to cross the 'shaky' bridge, has brought supporters from Portadown to Ballymacarrett for the match. The fans have left the train and may be seen in the background heading over Dee Street bridge to the ground. This overbridge had also spanned the closed BCDR main line to Comber and Newcastle. Portadown shed staff made the headboard from an old 'Bundoran Express' one which was lying at the back of the shed. Despite all these encouragements, Portadown lost 4-1 that day.** Derek Young

Bottom: **This happy shot was taken on 12th August 1965 at Victoria Park Halt. The grandstand at Glentoran's Oval football stadium can be seen in the distance. To the left of the picture are some of the 'prefab' houses built after the war to help alleviate the chronic housing shortage of those years. Many of these survived for much longer than they were intended to in various parts of the city and across the province. This was the year when the Belfast Central line was closed, cutting the Bangor branch off from the rest of the Irish railway system. It would be many years later before a steam locomotive would again make its way down the Bangor line. UG No 48 looks as if she is on a works train running wrong road.** Craig Robb

HOLYWOOD LOCALS

Above: **The County Down was probably the only Irish railway to declare that railmotors worked – indeed, it may well have been the only railway in these islands to make such a claim. They were certainly popular on the Belfast to Holywood line which was flat and posed few problems to these lightly powered units. No 1 is seen here at Holywood about to propel its coach back to Queens Quay. This is the smaller of the two sizes of coaches used. These machines helped the BCDR to hold its own with competing bus services and threats from Belfast Corporation to extend its tram routes. Behind the station is Holywood Gasworks which was a customer of the railway.** Ian Allan Library

Centre: **No 27 working a push-pull train at Holywood. Some of these services were extended to Craigavad which was another two miles beyond Holywood, where there was a crossover.** Drew Donaldson

Bottom: **Ireland's only four track main line! The new embankment on the Bangor side of Holywood had just been commissioned, allowing the roads authority to build a bypass without destroying the view of those houses along the front. This was the decision after a bitter fight by angry sea shore residents.** Richard Whitford

Above: At the time when some of the 'Jeeps' were being used on the Bangor line, on 2nd July 1952 we see WT class 2-6-4T No 10 climbing out of Holywood bound for the next stop at Marino. The train is made up of former NCC coaches. The second and fourth vehicles are noticeably wider than the other two. These were built to the Irish loading gauge, which was more generous that that which pertained across the Irish Sea. The other two are wartime replacements, built to the British loading gauge and distinctly narrower than their Irish cousins. S C Nash

Left: Climbing towards Craigavad, BCDR standard tank No 211 has a rather short train consisting of a mixture of bogie and six-wheeler stock. The spur which today leads to the Ulster Folk and Transport Museum was laid between the two bridges in the background. No 30 of this class is preserved in that museum. This peaceful scene belies the busy nature of the County Down's Bangor line which moved large numbers of commuters every weekday morning and evening and coped with equally large numbers travelling by excursion trains during the summer to enjoy the delights of the seaside at Bangor.

BANGOR WEST

Right: **One of the UTA's multi-engined railcar sets is seen passing Craigavad on its way to Bangor. These railcars were designed in the Duncrue Street workshops of the UTA and had Leyland 125hp engines, which made them similar to the GNR units. The big difference was in the control system which allowed multiple unit working and permitted any vehicle to be coupled to another no matter which direction they were pointing. The suspension may have been better but some of the old County Down coaches had more comfortable seats. One of the banner signals which were such a feature of the Bangor line for many years is clearly seen on the left of the picture.** Richard Whitford

Below: **On 1st September 1952, one of the large tanks, No 208, is seen arriving at a very rural Bangor West. A very different sight greets today's passengers as the area is almost totally built up. The catch point here was to protect against runaway vehicles on the deceptively steep gradient out of Bangor station, just a mile away.**
E M Patterson

Above: **On 14th May 1950, standard tank No 220 leaves Carnalea for Bangor West and then Bangor. This picture is very typical of the old BCDR, a small handsome tank engine pulling six wheeled Victorian coaches.** H C Casserley

Below: **Former GNR U class 4-4-0 No 65 (GNR No 200)** *Lough Melvin* **in blue livery approaches Bangor West with a return excursion to the Great Northern. In today's efficient railway system, with only the larger stations having the luxury of staff,**

Bangor West is the smallest station on NIR in which you may purchase a ticket and have the train door opened for you. Charles Friel collection

BANGOR

Above: **On 13th July 1964, steam and diesel sit side by side at Bangor. Alterations to the track layout (see page 61) have taken place. The scissors crossover has been replaced and the locomotive release road has been removed making the up platform, No 2, now the only one suitable for steam hauled excursions. The large water tank has disappeared but the sidings on the right, which were moved to allow the brick bus repair garage to be built, remain. Standing at the platform is UG No 48 (GNR No 146) with a heavy eight coach return excursion. A set of the MED diesel railcars which provided the normal passenger service on the Bangor line can be glimpsed at the other platform.** E M Patterson

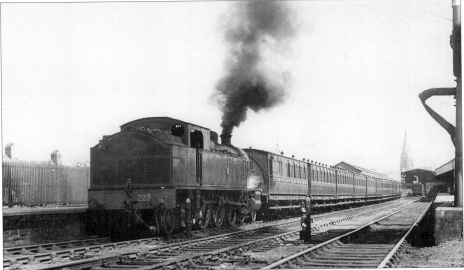

Centre: **In Ulster Transport times, Baltic tank No 223, with a Belfast bound train, is ready to begin what would be, for one of these engines, a slog back to Belfast. These unfortunate locomotives spent almost all their life on the Bangor line.** Charles Friel collection

Right: **GNR UG No 78 rests in the sun at the buffer stops at Bangor station she awaits the road to run round her train. The station has now been completely rebuilt with nothing of the original structure remaining. The facilities for the travelling public have been greatly enhanced in the process, with the bus station now adjacent to the railway station.** Charles Friel collection

Left: **At the buffer stops in Bangor, about to run round her train is No 26 dating from 1892, one of four 0-6-0s built by Beyer Peacock for the BCDR over the years. The company looked on these not as goods locomotives but as general purpose machines and they were used on all sorts of workings.** H C Casserley

Below: **No 67 (GNR No 202) *Louth* was one of the batch of U class 4-4-0s built by Beyer Peacock after the Second World War. Their square windowed cabs and higher set boiler gave them a slightly awkward look compared with the earlier engines which dated from 1915. However, they were a reliable and useful class.** Charles Friel collection

Opposite page:

Top: **On 12th March 1961, the ex-Great Northern steam crane No 3169, with UG No 48 (GNR No 146) in attendance, is at work on track alterations at Bangor station which involved replacement of the scissors crossover.** E M Patterson

Bottom: **PG No 100, pulls away from Bangor with a train of ex-NCC bogie suburban coaches which rather dwarf her.** Charles Friel collection

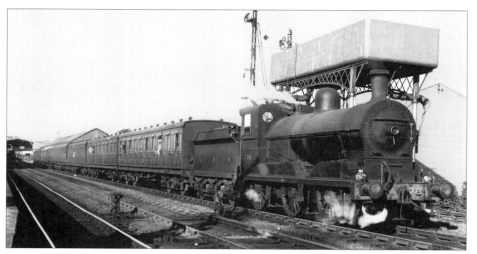

Top: **UG No 78 waits under the unusual water tank at Bangor. Generations of County Down drivers preferred to take water at Queens Quay rather than here or Donaghadee because they claimed the water was 'too hard'. The special about to leave mostly consists of the GNR's rather uncomfortable 100-seater K1 class low elliptical-roofed coaches. With their huge seating capacity, the operating department loved them, but the travelling public generally did not. The attractive BCDR signals behind the locomotive were later preserved by the Downpatrick Railway Museum.**

Centre: **UG No 80 prepares to depart with yet another excursion which includes some vintage ex-NCC straight-sided bogie vehicles. Over the years these workings brought a variety of steam working to the Bangor line and much business to the town. These ended when the line was cut off from the rest of the network in 1965.** Charles Friel collection

Below: **The GNR was always keen to promote excursion traffic. Here an almost brand new AEC express diesel unit, with a buffet car in the centre, almost certainly the Dublin based set used on the 'Enterprise', is leaving Bangor bound for Dublin on the return leg of a Saturday excursion. This set would normally lie idle at the weekends so it made good sense to press it into service for this working.** Desmond Coakham

RAILS THROUGH THE STREETS

CITY CENTRE SCENES

Above: **Horse trams running on 5ft 3in gauge track came to Belfast in the 1870s. In 1905, the system was electrified and converted to the British standard gauge of 4ft 8½in. The types of car used took the name of the general manager of the system when they were introduced. No 397, trundling past the City Hall, out of sight to the left of the photographer, was a Chamberlain car dating from 1930.**

Right: **No 434 seen in Donegall Place, was a McCreary car. On the left is the well-known store of Thorntons now alas no longer in existence, a mecca for young postwar vehicle collectors, which sold the first Dinky Toys to be produced after hostilities ceased.** Both Maybin collection

Above: **McCreary car No 397 leads a posse of trams past the City Hall**, out of sight on the left. Campbells coffee shop was housed in the white building immediately behind No 397. Campbells was a great institution occupying an old building which had settled down into a comfortable tilt. None of its walls were straight and the smell of roasting coffeee beans coming from it was haunting. The building just visible in the gap between the second and third tram is that rare creature, the private subscription library. The thriving Linenhall Library is still very much a part of Belfast life.

Below: **Built by Brush of Loughborough, the Chamberlain cars had such refinements as air brakes and electric heaters, altogether a most handsome vehicle. No 377 is in Wellington Place; the imposing building behind was the Belfast Technical College.**
Both, Maybin collection

Above: **This is Great Victoria Street with the Great Northern station in the background, with McCreary car No 430 turning into Howard Street. Behind her is the Hippodrome theatre and cinema long since gone but beside them is the Grand Opera House, now splendidly restored and** looking better than ever. **The large building with a fine array of chimneys behind the bus was the GNR Traffic Managers' office.**
Desmond Coakham

Below: **McCreary No 434 leads a long line of trams past St Anne's Cathedral, behind the** trees on the left in Donegall Street. A finelooking Rover 14 is taking advantage of a gap in the heavy traffic to cut into Academy Street. The trolleybus is unusual, probably a non standard Crossley rebuilt by the Belfast Corporation workshops.
R Brook, courtesy Maybin collection

TRAM DEPOTS

Left: **At Shore Road depot we see two of the cars built for the electrification of the system in 1905. The one on the left, No 89, was a one-off rebuild with the usual enclosed top deck, though unlike later rebuilds, the driver was left in the open. As can be imagined, No 89 was not popular with the drivers.** Kennedy collection

Bottom left: **No 249, seen here about to enter Sandy Row depot, was an interesting car. She was one of the horse trams selected for conversion to electric power but unlike No 246 (opposite page, bottom), she did not have a monitor roof, so conversion was not too difficult. A further distinguishing feature was the 'quarter turn' staircase, instead of the more usual 'half turn' type. No 249 has survived and can still be seen at the Ulster Folk & Transport Museum at Cultra.** Desmond Coakham

Bottom right: **No 78, seen at Mountpottinger depot in east Belfast, is another rebuild of a standard car. The top deck is completely glazed, but unlike most rebuilds, the windows on the top deck are the same depth all the way round. Compare this car with No 285 in the bottom picture on page 70.** Maybin collection

TRAM TYPES

Top: **McCreary car No 418 has stopped at one of the Fare Stages on the Lisburn Road. Woe betide if an Inspector caught you trying to travel further than your ticket allowed and into the next Fare Stage. Ordinary stopping places, as opposed to Fare Stages, were distinguished by a sign saying 'Stop'.** Maybin collection

Centre: **This is the terminus at the top of the Cliftonville Road where it joins the Oldpark Road. Nearest the camera is Chamberlain car No 364. Waiting for her to use the crossover is a Moffett car. These entered service in 1920/21 and were the first totally covered-in cars in the city. They must have been a great boon for travellers in the sometimes grim Belfast weather. There were quite a few tram routes in Belfast which had steepish inclines. On one famous occasion, a tram set off without the driver on board, gathering speed before leaving the tracks at the junction with the Antrim Road and ending up in a cobbler's shop. Fortunately, there were no injuries caused by this escapade.** Kennedy collection

Bottom: **Venerable old No 246 was a converted horse tram still doing rush hour service in 1947. Here she is being prepared to travel from Knock Road depot to Queens Road to help get the shipyard workers home. When the new red cars were ordered, on inspection it was found that many of the later horse drawn cars were in first class condition, being built of fine seasoned oak and mahogany. These were converted to electric traction. Some of the horse trams had an attractive curving clerestory-like monitor roof, so a distinguishing feature in some of the conversions was a layer with ventilators above the lower saloon quarterlights to cope with the extra height of the old roof. No 246 was one of the few horse tram conversions not to receive a covered-in top deck. In summer, with a few similar cars, she shuttled between the city centre and Bellevue Pleasure Gardens on the Antrim Road.** Desmond Coakham

SOUTH BELFAST ROUTES

Left: **Shaftesbury Square was a busy crossing point where the two outward bound routes to south Belfast destinations met. Trams travelled by both Great Victoria Street and Dublin Road/Bedford Street to reach their termini. A board in slots below a lower saloon window indicated which route was to be taken. Just visible in front of the NIRTB van is an Army canvas cabbed MW Bedford.** Maybin collection

Below: **Moffett car No 311 entering Bradbury Place passes a trailer carrying the fuselage of a Sunderland flying boat on its way from Short & Harland's works at the harbour to one of their satellite factories. The RUC man standing by the tram with his back to the camera has propped his BSA M20 motorbike nearby so as to enable him to sort the traffic problems. The tractor unit is an American-built Reo.** Bombardier

Top: **In another view of Bradbury Place, the tram tracks from the Lisburn Road trail in from the left. The tracks in front of the photographer lead to Malone and Stranmillis. The Belfast Central railway line runs almost under the cameraman's feet.** Desmond Coakham

Centre: **McCreary No 415 is loading at the stop opposite Queens University before heading for the Northern Counties station on York Road. Happily, the two storey houses on the left are still with us. However, a most attractive row of houses just peeking in on the left has been replaced by an ugly 1960s building housing the Students' Union.** R D S Wiseman, courtesy Maybin collection

Bottom: **This is University Road at the point where it divides into the Stranmillis Road on the right and the Malone Road. Chamberlain No 358 is heading up the Stranmillis Road while a Hillman Minx seems to be wandering lost across the road towards the entrance to Methodist College or Methody as it is always called. The middle shop was a Post Office run by a genial man called Ron Robinson who in his spare time ran a small model railway business. In its heyday, it was a haven for enthusiasts.** Desmond Coakham

Opposite page:

Top: **This is the Malone Road tram terminus in this very upmarket leafy suburb of south Belfast. Despite the affluence of the area, where there were probably many more car owners than in most other parts of the city, there were still plenty of tram patrons. The two car family was still a long way off so if there was a car in a household, the men would probably be the drivers, leaving the womenfolk to take the tram!** Kennedy collection

Bottom: **This is Stranmillis terminus with the River Lagan behind and just out of sight on the right, the first lock on the Lagan Navigation. There is now a popular public house called 'Cutters Wharf' at this spot. No 285 is typical of the rebuilds of the early open-top electric cars distinguished by the deeper windows in the middle of the top deck.** Kennedy collection

This page:

Top: **McCreary No 426 waits at Balmoral terminus to trundle over the crossover and travel across the city to Ligoniel. Close by is Balmoral station on the Great Northern's main line. There seemed to be enough business for both train and tram, although the railway couldn't match the frequency of the trams.** R Brook, courtesy Maybin collection

Centre: **No 22, a Standard Red rebuild of 1905, stands on the Lisburn Road at Marlborough Park. This was a short working used during busy times. Balmoral terminus was a mile further up the road. The Smyth & McClure store on the left of the picture was part of an early chain of grocery chain shops, in the days long before supermarkets were heard of in Northern Ireland.** Maybin collection

Bottom: **A line-up of trams at Balmoral terminus with the Kings Hall of the Royal Ulster Agricultural Society behind. During show weeks the trams were very busy, as was nearby Balmoral station.** A D Packer, courtesy Maybin collection

TRAMS IN EAST BELFAST

Above: **Rebuild No 266 with a squadron of McCreary cars follow a Daimler bus as they inch past the County Down terminus on the slow haul from the shipyard to the city centre and beyond. In September 1953 when this photograph was taken the amount of tram traffic had diminished from the days when the cars bulged to overflow with the numbers being carried.**
A D Packer, courtesy Maybin collection

Below: **Two McCreary cars trundling along the Albertbridge Road – a rather narrow thoroughfare for so much traffic. The attractive gas lights which Belfast seemed to retain after other cities changed to electricity are still providing light, but the tram now takes its power from a trolleybus wire; times are changing. The date is uncertain but with sun awnings over the shops and flags out it's most likely to be a few days before 12th of July.**
R D S Wiseman, courtesy Maybin collection

Opposite page:

Top left: **This is the peaceful terminus of the Bloomfield route in east Belfast in the 1930s. Today there is a busy roundabout at this spot. Rebuild 254 would not feel at home now if she came back to this location.**
John Kennedy collection

Top right: **No 164 is a rebuild from a Standard Red tram. This work was carried out locally and the lower original windows in the centre section of the upper saloon make these cars easy to spot. She is standing across the 5ft 3in track of the Harbour Railway which ran from the BCDR at Queens Quay station to the coal quay and connected with Harland & Wolff's works tramway. Behind in the distance is the enormous floating crane which was once employed to transport NCC Moguls across the harbour from York Road to Harland & Wolff for refitting after the end of the Second World War, a spectacle illustrated in another title in this series. (See *The LMS In Ireland*, Midland Publishing, 2000, pages 40 and 41)**
Desmond Coakham

Bottom: **A line of trams on Queens Road waiting to handle the rush of shipyard workers heading home at 5.30pm. During the Second World War Harland & Wolff employed up to 30,000 men.**
Maybin collection

Left: **A scene at Mountpottinger with a McCreary car on her way from Castlereagh to the city centre. The trolleybus in the background is on the Albertbridge Road. The tram depot was 50 yards further on. This photograph was taken before the Castlereagh route was converted to trolleybus operation and the tram route closed except the spur into the depot.** Maybin collection

Below: **The world's largest ropeworks is on the right as a Chamberlain car is negotiating a newly installed chord which will take her into the Newtownards Road from the Albertbridge Road and thence to Queens Road. The introduction of trolleybuses on the Castlereagh Road services which went past Mountpottinger tram depot and the lifting of tram tracks in Castlereagh Street, where the depot was located, was the reason for the long detour faced by No 360. The picture was taken in August 1952.** R Brook, courtesy Maybin collection

NORTH BELFAST

Right: **McCreary car No 405 is travelling past the offices and printing works of** *The Northern Whig*, **a newspaper which has not been published for many years, although the building has been pleasantly restored.**

Below: **The longest route on the Belfast tramway system terminated at Glengormley on the northern edge of the city, a distance of about five and a half miles. The final two miles were single line with passing loops. The Glen Hotel was rebuilt as a pub after being destroyed by a terrorist bomb during the recent 'troubles'. Both, Maybin collection**

Above: **Belfast Corporation purchased** *Jean* **(known previously as** *The Bug***) in 1934 from the famous Romney Hythe & Dymchurch Railway in Kent. Built by the German firm of Krauss in 1926 as an 0-4-0 tender locomotive of 15in gauge, she shuttled between two stations in Bellevue** Pleasure Gardens, passing through the maintenance shed, which became a sort of a tunnel. At each end she trundled round a loop for the return journey. Shortly after the end of the Second World War the line was closed after a landslip covered part of the trackbed. Charles Friel collection

Below: **After spending many years lying in a local scrap yard** *Jean* **was rescued and is now restored and back home on the RHDR.** Charles Friel collection

Opposite page:

Top: **In this 1930s view, Standard Red No 10 is on the Old Park Road, while the other trams are on the Crumlin Road. No 353 is heading to the Ulster Cricket grounds on the Ormeau Road, suggesting that this is a Saturday.** John Kennedy collection

Bottom: **No 406 was Belfast's last new type of tram. Introduced in 1934 and designed by the general manager Lt-Col R McCreary, the bodies were mostly locally built with running gear from Hurst Nelson in Scotland. They were the first cars with folding doors. Unfortunately, this useful contribution to comfort in our difficult climate did not benefit the passengers since those being used for boarding and leaving were never closed, though the driver's comfort was increased dramatically by their use. No 406 has just left the Ligoniel terminus and is about to descend the steep hill towards the Crumlin Road and the city centre.** Patrick L Cassidy

Above: **York Street station in the 1930s with 'Standard Red' car No 2 emerging from the spur into the station concourse on a working to Castle Junction in the city centre. This interesting example of integrated transport was particularly welcome in Belfast's inclement weather. On the right of the picture, in Whitla Street, Chamberlain car No 389 has arrived on a short working and is standing outside the entrance to the Midland Hotel, its trolley pole already transferred to the other overhead wire prior to trundling over the crossover for the return journey.**
John Kennedy collection

Left: **The Queens Quay station of the Belfast & County Down railway also had a tram spur from the Queens Road route which ran into the concourse. Here Moffett car No 314 leaves the station for the city centre.**
Desmond Coakham

THE RUBBER TYRED 'TRAM'

Right: **Trolleybuses arrived in Belfast on 28th March 1938 and ran on the Falls Road route, where they became immensely popular. Extra vehicles were ordered but the outbreak of war delayed delivery until 1940. AEC No 95 was one of this batch. It will travel past York Road station to terminate at the Grove Baths. This was a short working on the Shore Road route; most trolleybuses went on to either Whitewell or Whitehouse. No 95 was photographed on 5th October 1963 in Donegall Place with the City Hall behind.**

Below: **This view looks towards Castle Junction, the hub of the trolleybus system. No 162, bound for Cregagh, was built by Guy and entered service in 1948. All new Belfast vehicles had bodies manufactured by the local firm of Harkness, including the Daimler motorbus behind. Belfast trolleybuses operated under local statutes which treated them as if they were part of the tramway system. They did not need Public Service Vehicle certificates, nor did their drivers need ordinary road driving licences. It also allowed them to be built to a much greater length than contemporary diesel buses.** Both, Richard Whitford

Above: **These three well turned out trolleybuses in North Queen Street are travelling on a loop which will take them either back up the Falls Road or, in the case of the second bus, out to the Cliftonville Road. No 217 is from the last batch built and sports a sliding door to the driver's cab and other refinements which made them look very up to date at the time. The entire system closed on Sunday 12th May 1968 after a relatively short if successful life. The** trolleybuses were reliable, fast and quiet and were free of the pollution associated with the internal combustion engine.

Below: **On 9th May 1964, one of the final batch of buses crosses the junction between the Antrim Road, Limestone Road and Cavehill Road. No 233 was built by BUT, the company also responsible for the final batch of GNRB railcars. The Antrim Road route to Glengormley, which was** almost in the country in those days, was the longest on the system. The Cavehill Road, although an important diesel bus route, was never served by either trams or trolleybuses. The Cavehill mineral railway, which dated back to the 1830s, ran close to this location. Whilst all material traces of this line have disappeared, visitors to the Ulster Folk & Transport Museum can still see No 233, which has been preserved there. Both, Richard Whitford